Algernon Charles Swinburne

A Note on Charlotte Brontë

Algernon Charles Swinburne

A Note on Charlotte Brontë

ISBN/EAN: 9783337142070

Printed in Europe, USA, Canada, Australia, Japan

Cover: Foto ©ninafisch / pixelio.de

More available books at **www.hansebooks.com**

A NOTE
ON
CHARLOTTE BRONTË

WORKS BY MR. SWINBURNE.

The Queen Mother and Rosamond. Fcp. 8vo. 5s.

Atalanta in Calydon. A New Edition. Crown 8vo. 6s.

Chastelard: A Tragedy. Fcp. 8vo. 7s.

Poems and Ballads. Fcp. 8vo. 9s.

Notes on 'Poems and Ballads.' 8vo. 1s.

William Blake. A Critical Essay. With Facsimile Paintings. Demy 8vo. 16s.

Songs before Sunrise. Crown 8vo. 10s. 6d.

Bothwell: A Tragedy. Two Vols. crown 8vo. 12s. 6d.

George Chapman. An Essay. Crown 8vo. 7s.

Songs of Two Nations. Crown 8vo. 6s.

Essays and Studies. Crown 8vo. 12s.

Erechtheus: A Tragedy. Crown 8vo. 6s.

Note of an English Republican on the Muscovite Crusade. 8vo. 1s.

CHATTO & WINDUS, Piccadilly, W.

A NOTE

ON

CHARLOTTE BRONTË

BY

ALGERNON CHARLES SWINBURNE

London
CHATTO & WINDUS, PICCADILLY
1877

All rights reserved

LONDON: PRINTED BY
SPOTTISWOODE AND CO., NEW-STREET SQUARE
AND PARLIAMENT STREET

TO

My Friend

THEODORE WATTS

I dedicate this study; an inadequate acknowledgment of much personal obligation, and an imperfect expression of fellow-feeling on the subject here imperfectly and inadequately handled.

A. C. S.

A NOTE

ON

CHARLOTTE BRONTË.

THE priceless contribution to our knowledge of one of the greatest among women, for which the thanks of all students who have at heart the honour of English literature are due to Mr. Wemyss Reid, had on its first appearance the singular good fortune to evoke from a weekly paper of much literary and philosophic pretension one of the most profound and memorable remarks ever put forth even in the columns of the contemporary *Spectator*. On the 11th of November, 1876, there appeared in that quarter a written assurance that its literary critic did actually 'agree with this biographer' in thinking that the works of Charlotte Brontë 'will one day again be regarded as evidences of exceptional intellectual power.' The present writer for once feels himself emboldened to express in his turn his own agreement with this critic in the opinion that they not impossibly may; he will even venture to avow his humble conviction that they may with no great show of unreason be expected to outlive the works of some few at least among the female immortals of whom the happy present hour is so more than seasonably prolific; to be read with delight and wonder, and re-read with reverence and admiration, when darkness everlasting has long since fallen upon all human memory of their cheap scientific, their vulgar erotic, and their voluminous domestic schools; when even 'Daniel Deronda' has gone the way of all waxwork, when even Miss Broughton no longer cometh up as a flower, and even Mrs. Oliphant is at length cut down like the grass. It is under the rash and reckless impulse of this unfashionable belief that I would offer a superfluous word or two of remark on the twin-born genius of the less mortal sisters who left with us for ever the legacies of 'Jane Eyre' and 'Wuthering Heights.'

The one sovereign quality common alike to the spirit and the work of these two great women, whose names make up with Mrs. Browning's the perfect trinity for England of highest female fame, is one which even the prodigal Genius or God who presided at her birth could not or would not accord to the passionate and lyric-minded poetess. It is possibly the very rarest of all powers or faculties of imagination applied to actual life and individual character; I can trace it in no living English authoress one half so strongly or so clearly marked as in the work of the illustrious and honoured lady—honoured scarcely more by admiration from some quarters than by obloquy from others—to whom we owe the over-true story of 'Joshua Davidson,' and the worthiest tribute ever yet paid to the memory of Walter Savage Landor. But in

Charlotte and Emily Brontë this innate personal quality was manifested, as far as my knowledge or power of comparison extends, at a quite incomparable degree of excellence; of perfection, I would have written, but for the fear of giving too Irish a turn to the parting phrase of my sentence. It is a quality as hard to define as impossible to mistake; even the static and dynamic terms of definition so freely and scientifically misused in the latest school of feminine romance would scarcely help us much towards an adequate apprehension or expression of it. But its absence or its presence is or should be anywhere and always recognisable at a glance, whether dynamic or merely static, of a skilful or unskilful eye to discern the systole from the diastole of human companionship—or even of inhuman jargon. The crudest as the most refined pedantry of semi-science, tricked out at second hand in the freshest or the stalest phrases of archaic schoolmen or neologic lecturers that may be swept up from the dustiest boards or picked up under the daintiest platforms irradiated or obfuscated by new lamps or old, will avail nothing to guide any possible seeker on the path towards an exploration by physical analysis or metaphysical synthesis of the source or the process, the fountain or the channel or the issue, of this subtle and infallible force of nature—the progress from the root into the fruit of this direct creative instinct. Yet thus far, perhaps, we may reasonably attempt some indication of the difference which divides pure genius from mere intellect as by a great gulf fixed; the quality of the latter, we may say, is constructive, the property of the former is creative. Adam Bede, for instance, or even Tito Melema, is an example of construction—and the latter is one of the finest in literature; Edward Rochester and Paul Emanuel are creations. And the inevitable test or touchstone of this indefinable difference is the immediate and enduring impression set at once and engraved for ever on the simplest or the subtlest mind of the most careless or the most careful student. In every work of pure genius we feel while it is yet before us—and if we cease for a little to feel when out of sight of it for awhile, we surely feel afresh each time our sight of it is renewed—the sense of something inevitable, some quality incorporate and innate, which determines that it shall be thus and not otherwise; and we need not the 'illative sense' of Dr. Newman's invention to teach us 'the grammar of assent' to the matter proposed to us as subject or as object for our imaginative belief. Belief, and not assent, it is that we give to the highest.

There is no surer test as there can be no higher evidence than this of that imperative and primary genius which holds its power in fee of no other mind, which derives of no foreign stream through the conduit of no alien channel. Perhaps we may reasonably divide all imaginative work into three classes; the lowest, which leaves us in a complacent mood of acquiescence with the graceful or natural inventions and fancies of an honest and ingenious workman, and in no mind to question or dispute the accuracy of his transcript from life or the fidelity of his design to the modesty and the likelihood of nature; the second, of high enough quality to engage our judgment in its service, and make direct demand on our grave attention for deliberate assent or dissent; the third, which in the exercise of its highest faculties at their best neither solicits nor seduces nor provokes us to acquiescence or demur, but compels us without question to positive acceptance and belief. Of the first class it would be superfluous to cite instances from among writers of our own day, not undeserving of serious respect and of genuine gratitude for much honest work done and honest pleasure conferred on us. Of the second order our literature has no more apt and brilliant examples than George Eliot and George Meredith. Of the third, if in such a matter as this I may trust my own instinct—that last resource and ultimate reason of all critics in every case and on every question — there is no clearer and more positive instance in the whole world of letters than that supplied by the genius of Charlotte Brontë.

I do not mean that such an instance is to be found in the treatment of each figure in each of her great three books. If this could accurately be said, it could not reasonably be denied that she might justly claim and must naturally assume that seat by the side of Shakespeare which certain critics of the hour are prompt alike to assign alternately to the author of 'Adam Bede' and to the author of 'Queen Mary.' Only in the eyes of such critics as these, or in the glassy substitutes which serve their singular kind as proxies for a human squint, will it seem to imply a want of serious interest and respect in the former direction, of loyal and grateful admiration in the latter, if I confess that to my unaided organs and limited capacities of sight the one comparison appears as portentously farcical as the other in its superhuman or subsimious absurdity; that I should find it as hard an article of religion to digest and assimilate into the body of a living faith, which bade me believe in the assumption of the goddess as that which bade me believe in the ascension of the god to complete the co-eternal and co-equal personality of English genius at its highest apogee, in its triune and bisexual apotheosis. But, without putting in a claim for the author of 'Jane Eyre' as qualified to ascend the height on which a minority of not overwise admirers would fain enthrone a demigoddess of more dubious divinity than hers, I must take leave to reiterate my conviction that no living English or female writer can rationally be held her equal in what I cannot but regard as the highest and the rarest quality which supplies the hardest and the surest proof of a great and absolute genius for the painting and the handling of human characters in mutual relation and reaction. Even the glorious mistress of all forms and powers of imaginative prose, who has lately left France afresh in mourning— even George Sand herself had not this gift in like measure with those great twin sisters in genius who were born to the stern and strong-hearted old Rector of Haworth.

The gift of which I would speak is that of a power to make us feel in every nerve, at every step forward which our imagination is compelled to take under the guidance of another's, that thus and not otherwise, but in all things altogether even as we are told and shown, it was and it must have been with the human figures set before us in their action and their suffering; that thus and not otherwise they absolutely must and would have felt and thought and spoken under the proposed conditions. It is something for a writer to have achieved if he has made it worth our fancy's while to consider by the light of imaginative reason whether the creatures of his own fancy would in actual fact and life have done as he has made them do or not; it is something, and by comparison it is much. But no definite terms of comparison will suffice to express how much more than this it is to have done what the youngest of capable readers must feel on first opening 'Jane Eyre' that the writer of its very first pages has shown herself competent to do. In almost all other great works of its kind, in almost all the sovereign masterpieces even of Fielding, of Thackeray, of the royal and imperial master, Sir Walter

Scott himself—to whose glorious memory I need offer no apology for the attribution of epithets which I cannot but regret to remember that even in their vulgar sense he would not have regarded as other than terms of honour—even in the best and greatest works of these our best and greatest we do not find this one great good quality so innate, so immanent as in hers. At most we find the combination of event with character, the coincidence of action with disposition, the coherence of consequences with emotions, to be rationally credible and acceptable to the natural sense of a reasonable faith. We rarely or never feel that, given the characters, the incidents become inevitable; that such passion must needs bring forth none other than such action, such emotions cannot choose but find their only issue in such events. And certainly we do not feel, what it seems to me the highest triumph of inspired intelligence and creative instinct to succeed in making us feel, that the mainspring of all, the central relation of the whole, 'the very pulse of the machine,' has in it this occult inexplicable force of nature. But when Catherine Earnshaw says to Nelly Dean, 'I *am* Heathcliff!' and when Jane Eyre answers Edward Rochester's question, whether she feels in him the absolute sense of fitness and correspondence to herself which he feels to himself in her, with the words which close and crown the history of their twin-born spirits—'To the finest fibre of my nature, sir'—we feel to the finest fibre

of our own that these are no mere words.
On this ground at least it might for once
be not unpardonable to borrow their standing reference or illustration from that comparative school of critics whose habit of comparison we have treated with something less than respect, and say, as was said on another score of Emily Brontë in particular by Sydney Dobell, in an admirable paper which we miss with regret and with surprise from among the costly relics of his genius, so lovingly set in order and so ably lighted up by the faithful friendship and the loyal intelligence of Professor Nichol —that either sister in this single point 'has done no less' than Shakespeare. As easily might we imagine a change of the mutual relations between the characters of Shake-

speare as a corresponding revolution or reversal of conditions among theirs.

If I turn again for contrast or comparison with their works to the work of George Eliot, it will be attributed by no one above the spiritual rank and type of Pope's representative dunces to irreverence or ingratitude for the large and liberal beneficence of her genius at its best. But she alone among our living writers is generally admitted or assumed as the rightful occupant, or at least as the legitimate claimant, of that foremost place in the front rank of artists in this kind which none can hold or claim without challenging such comparison or such contrast. And in some points it is undeniable that she may claim precedence, not of these alone, but of all other illustrious women. Such wealth and depth of thoughtful and fruitful humour, of vital and various intelligence, no woman has ever shown—no woman perhaps has ever shown a tithe of it. In knowledge, in culture, perhaps in capacity for knowledge and for culture, Charlotte Brontë was no more comparable to George Eliot than George Eliot is comparable to Charlotte Brontë in purity of passion, in depth and ardour of feeling, in spiritual force and fervour of forthright inspiration. It would be rather a rough and sweeping than a loose or inaccurate division which should define the one as a type of genius distinguished from intellect, the other of intellect as opposed to genius. But it would, as I venture to think, be little or nothing more or less than accurate to recognise in George Eliot a type of intelligence vivified and coloured by a vein of genius, in Charlotte Brontë a type of genius directed and moulded by the touch of intelligence. No better test of this distinction could be desired than a comparison of their respective shortcomings or failures. These will serve, by their difference in kind and import, in quality and in weight, to show the depth and width of the great gulf between pure genius and pure intellect, even better than a comparison of their highest merits and achievements.

That great genius is liable to great error the world has ever been willing, if not more than willing, to admit; that great genius not equally balanced by great intellect is not one half as liable to go one half as wrong as intellect unequally counterpoised by genius, is a truth less popular and less familiar, but neither less important nor less indisputable. That Charlotte Brontë, a woman of the first order of genius, could go very wrong indeed, there are whole scenes and entire characters in her work which afford more than ample proof. But George Eliot, a woman of the first order of intellect, has once and again shown how much further and more steadily and more hopelessly and more irretrievably and more intolerably wrong it is possible for mere intellect to go than it ever can be possible for mere genius. Having no taste for the dissection of dolls, I shall leave Daniel Deronda in his natural place above the ragshop door; and having no ear for the melodies of a Jew's harp, I shall leave the Spanish Gipsy to perform on that instrument to such audience as she may collect. It would be unjust and impertinent to dwell much on Charlotte Brontë's brief and modest attempts in verse; but it would be unmanly and unkindly to touch at all on George Eliot's; except indeed to remark in passing that they are about equally commendable for the one and for the other of those negative good qualities which I have commended in Miss Brontë's. And from this point of difference, if from no other point here discernible, those who will or who can learn anything may learn a lesson in criticism which may perhaps be worth laying to heart: that genius, though it can put forth no better claim than intellect may assert for itself to share the papal gift of infallibility, is naturally the swifter of the two to perceive and to retrieve its errors. Where genius takes one false step in the twilight and draws back by instinct, intelligence once misguided will take a thousand without the slightest diffidence; will put its best foot foremost in the pitchy darkness, step out gallantly through all brakes and quagmires till stuck fast up to the middle, and higher yet, in some blind Serbonian bog of blundering presumption, and thence will not improbably strike up a psalm of hoarse thanksgiving or shrill self-gratulation, to be echoed from afar by the thousand marshy throats of a Mæotian or Bœotian frog concert, for the grace here given it to have set a triumphant foot on the solid rock, and planted a steady flagstaff on the splendid summits of supreme and unsurpassable success.

But we will follow neither the brief excursions of tentative and self-distrustful genius, nor the long aberrations of belated and self-confident intelligence, across any line of country never made for them to traverse and return with any trophies of the chase. Britomartis or Bradamante, on her most desperate and forlorn adventure, has a claim at least on the compassionate forbearance of every good knight-errant who may have ridden on the like or any such other quest; and even the felon Sir Breuse Sans Pitié might be moved by some momentary throb of chivalrous condolence at the pitiful and unseemly spectacle of an Amazon thrown sprawling over the crupper of her spavined and spur-galled Pegasus. It is on ground proper to either or common to both that we will compare the pace and action, the blood and the wind and the staying power, of either steed entered for this race. And first we will examine, dropping our equine metaphor before we have ridden it to death, what may be the very gravest flaws or shortcomings perceptible in the work of Charlotte Brontë. So doing, I believe that any loyal and capable critic will as surely find as he will joyfully admit that her failures never affect the central and radical quality of that work. The heart of it is always whole; its outskirts or extremities alone, perhaps only its dress and decorations, are in any degree impaired. Take the first work of her genius in its ripe fullness and freshness of new fruit; a twig or two is twisted or blighted of the noble tree, a bud or so has been nipped or cankered by adverse winds or frost; but root and branch and bole are all straight and strong and solid and sound in grain. Whatever in 'Jane Eyre' is other than good is also less than important. The accident which brings a famished wanderer to the door of unknown kinsfolk might be a damning flaw in a novel of mere incident; but incident is not the keystone and commonplace is not the touchstone of this. The vulgar insolence and brutish malignity of the well-born guests at Thornfield Hall are grotesque and incredible in speakers of their imputed station; these are the natural properties of that class of persons which then supplied, as it yet supplies, the writers of such articles as one of memorable infamy and imbecility on 'Jane Eyre' to the artistic and literary department of the 'Quarterly Review.' So gross and grievous a blunder would entail no less than ruin on a mere novel of manners; but accuracy in the distinction and reproduction of social characteristics is not the test of capacity for such work as this. That test is only to be found in the grasp and manipulation of manly and womanly character. And, to my mind, the figure of Edward Rochester in this book remains, and seems like to remain, one of the only two male figures of wholly truthful workmanship and vitally heroic mould ever carved and coloured by a woman's hand. The other it is superfluous to mention; all possible readers will have uttered before I can transcribe the name of Paul Emanuel.

And now we must regretfully and respectfully consider of what quality and what kind may be the faults which deform the best and ripest work of Charlotte Brontë's chosen rival. Few or none, I should suppose, of her most passionate and intelligent admirers would refuse to accept 'The Mill on the Floss' as on the whole at once the highest and the purest and the fullest example of her magnificent and matchless powers—for matchless altogether, as I have already insisted, they undoubtedly are in their own wide and fruitful field of work. The first two-thirds of the book suffice to compose perhaps the very noblest of tragic as well as of humorous prose idyls in the language; comprising, as they likewise do, one of the sweetest as well as saddest and tenderest as well as subtlest examples of dramatic analysis—a study in that kind as soft and true as Rousseau's, as keen and true as Browning's, as full as either's of the fine and bitter sweetness of a pungent and fiery fidelity. But who can forget the horror of inward collapse, the sickness of spiritual reaction, the reluctant incredulous rage of disenchantment and disgust, with which he first came upon the thrice unhappy third part? The two first volumes have all the intensity and all the perfection of George Sand's best work, tempered by all the simple purity and interfused with all the stainless pathos of Mrs.

Gaskell's; they carry such affluent weight of thought and shine with such warm radiance of humour as invigorates and illuminates the work of no other famous woman; they have the fiery clarity of crystal or of lightning; they go near to prove a higher claim and attest a clearer right on the part of their author than that of George Sand herself to the crowning crown of praise conferred on her by the hand of a woman even greater and more glorious than either in her sovereign gift of lyric genius, to the salutation given as by an angel indeed from heaven, of 'large-brained woman and large-hearted man.' And the fuller and deeper tone of colour combined with greater sharpness and precision of outline may be allowed to excuse the apparent amount of obligation—though we may hardly see how this can be admitted to explain the remarkable reticence which reserves all acknowledgment and dissembles all consciousness of that sufficiently palpable and weighty and direct obligation—to Mrs. Gaskell's beautiful story of 'The Moorland Cottage'; in which not the identity of name alone, nor only their common singleness of heart and simplicity of spirit, must naturally recall the gentler memory of the less high-thoughted and high-reaching heroine to the warmest and the worthiest admirers of the later-born and loftier-minded Maggie; though the hardness and brutality of the baser brother through whom she suffers be the outcome in manhood as in childhood of mere greedy instinct and vulgar egotism, while the full eventual efflorescence of the same gracious qualities in Tom Tulliver is tracked with incomparable skill and unquestionable certitude of touch to the far other root of sharp narrow self-devotion and honest harsh self-reliance.

'So far, all honour;' as Phraxanor says of Joseph in the noble poem of Mr. Wells. But what shall any one say of the upshot? If we are really to take it on trust, to confront it as a contingent or conceivable possibility, resting our reluctant faith on the authority of so great a female writer, that a woman of Maggie Tulliver's kind can be moved to any sense but that of bitter disgust and sickening disdain by a thing—I will not write, a man—of Stephen

Guest's; if we are to accept as truth and fact, however astonishing and revolting, so shameful an avowal, so vile a revelation as this; in that ugly and lamentable case, our only remark, as our only comfort, must be that now at least the last word of realism has surely been spoken, the last abyss of cynicism has surely been sounded and laid bare. The three master cynics of French romance are eclipsed and distanced and extinguished, passed over and run down and snuffed out on their own boards. To the rosy innocence of Laclos, to the cordial optimism of Stendhal, to the trustful tenderness of Mérimée, no such degradation of female character seems ever to have suggested itself as imaginable. Iago never flung such an imputation on all womanhood; Madame de Merteuil would never have believed it. For a higher view and a more cheering aspect of the sex, we must turn back to these gentler teachers, these more flattering painters of our own; we must take up 'La Double Méprise'—or 'Le Rouge et le Noir'—or 'Les Liaisons Dangereuses.'

But I for one am not prepared or willing to embrace a belief so much too degrading and depressing for the conception of those pure and childlike souls. My faith will not digest at once the first two volumes and the third volume of 'The Mill on the Floss'; my conscience or credulity has not gorge enough for such a gulp. Whatever capacity for belief is in me I find here impaled once more as on the horns of that old divine's dilemma between the irreconcilable attributes of goodness and omnipotence in the supposed Creator of suffering and of sin. If the one quality be predicable, the other quality cannot be predicable of the same subject. As between κοινὴ and ποινὴ, we must choose. Lady Percy on the lap of Falstaff, bidding him patch up his old body for heaven; Miranda nestling in the arms of Trinculo; Virgilia seeking consolation for her husband's exile in the rival devotion of Brutus and Sicinius; Desdemona finding refuge from her troubles on the bosom of Roderigo—could no longer pretend to be the widow of Hotspur, the bride of Ferdinand, the wife of the noblest Roman, the fellow-martyr of the nobler Moor. No higher tribute can be claimed and no deeper condemnation can be incurred by perverse or intermittent genius than is conveyed or implied in such comparisons as these. The hideous transformation by which Maggie is debased—were it but for an hour—into the willing or yielding companion of Stephen's flight would probably and deservedly have been resented as a brutal and vulgar outrage on the part of a male novelist. But the man never lived, I do believe, who could have done such a thing as this: as the man, I should suppose, does not exist who could make for the first time the acquaintance of Mr. Stephen Guest with no incipient sense of a twitching in his fingers and a tingling in his toes at the notion of any contact between Maggie Tulliver and a cur so far beneath the chance of promotion to the notice of his horsewhip, or elevation to the level of his boot.

Here then is the patent flaw, here too plainly is the flagrant blemish, which defaces and degrades the very crown and flower of George Eliot's wonderful and most noble work; no rent or splash on the raiment, no speck or scar on the skin of it, but a cancer in the very bosom, a gangrene in the very flesh. It is a radical and mortal plague-spot, corrosive and incurable; in the apt and accurate phrase of Rabelais, 'an enormous solution of continuity.' The book is not the same before it and after. No washing or trimming, no pruning or purging, could eradicate or efface it; it could only be removable by amputation and remediable by cautery. It is even a worse offence against ethics, a more grievous insult to the moral sentiment or sense, because more deliberate and elaborate, than the two actual and unpardonable sins of Shakespeare: the menace of unnatural marriage between Oliver and Celia, and again between Isabella and her 'old fantastical duke of dark corners.' Scandalous and injurious as these vile suggestions are, they are yet but as hasty blots dropped by an impatient hand, as crude excrescences which may be pared and leave no scar, as broken hints of a bad dream which the waking memory may be fain and able to forget, to shake off it and be clean again; retaining no thought of Rosalind's cousin but as she first came into the forest of Arden, of Claudio's sister but as she first was enrolled among the votarists of St. Clare.

Far otherwise it is with the poor noble heroine so strangely disgraced and discrowned of natural honour by the strong and cruel hand which created her; and which could not redeem or raise her again, even by the fittest and noblest of all deaths conceivable, from the mire of ignominy into which it had been pleased to cast her down or bid her slip at the beck and call of a counter-jumping Antinous, a Lauzun of the counting-house, as vulgar as Vivien and as mean as the fellow who could gloat on the prospective degradation and anticipated unhappiness of a woman he forsooth had loved, under the wholly impossible condition of an utterly unimaginable hypothesis that the unfortunate young lady, who had at least the good fortune to escape the miserable ignominy of union with such a kinsman, might have declined on a range of lower feelings and a narrower heart than his; a supposition, as most men would think, beyond the power of omnipotence itself to realise. Surely our world would seem in danger of forgetting, under the guidance and example of its most brilliant literary chiefs, that there are characters and emotions which may not lie beyond the limits of degraded nature, but do assuredly grovel beneath the notice of undegenerate art; and that of such, most unquestionably,—if any such there be—are the characters and emotions of such reptile amorists as debase by the indecent exposure of their dastardly and rancorous egotism the moral value of such otherwise admirable masterpieces as 'Locksley Hall' and 'The Mill on the Floss.' An eminent historian, notable alike as a reviler of Frenchmen and a champion of Bulgarians, has written a paper to show that the law of honour as understood by our forefathers is an obsolete and artificial invention of depraved or barbarous times; an opinion which may help to explain, if not to justify, his national antipathies and sympathies; and some at least among our living elders in the field of imaginative letters would seem to have adopted, with more than historic ardour, a creed which nullifies the foolish traditions and explodes the simple doctrines of superstitious chivalry. Yet I for one, though not like to feel personally aggrieved or even ungratified by the most extravagant of English compliments addressed to France, should be sorry to suppose that it was even yet a taste exclusively reserved for men with French blood in their veins or French sympathies in their hearts, to prefer the old-world principle of mere chivalrous loyalty, of passion self-sacrificed and self-forgetting woman-worship, of knightly folly and faith shown even in the service of a lawless love —or lawless but for the law of honour, that worn-out spiritual mainspring and worthless moral motive of 'art with poisonous honey stolen from France'—to all the home-made treacle of the Laureate's morality. Poisonous as to certain tastes may be the

natural passions condoned or consecrated
by chivalry, and preposterous in certain
eyes as are the conventional principles es-
tablished or confirmed by its law, I am not
reluctant, on behalf of the nation and its
creed, to admit that it would be no less
difficult to derive from a French origin or
refer to a French example the taint of such
a distemper as is implied by this distaste,
than to inoculate with its infection the spirit
of a Frenchman or a gentleman.

No outrage of this kind on womanly loyalty
and manly instinct was among the possible
errors of Charlotte Brontë's heroic soul. To
errors of some gravity that great spirit was
indeed liable on more lines than one; her
critical judgment, for instance, on Mr. Tenny-

son's 'In Memoriam' was almost as grotesque in its ineptitude as that of M. Taine's very self; and under the gigantic shadow of Balzac's many-featured and colossal empire she would seem, like many if not most Englishwomen, to have come in as it were on the wrong side. The critical faculty in a woman of genius, if not well trained and cultivated with much labour of spiritual husbandry, seems naturally more prone to such flaws and lapses than the learned judgment of an intelligence duly warmed by the suns and watered by the streams of wide and fertilising study can ever claim the slightest excuse or plead the slightest apology for having shown itself at any time to be. Nor can we say that Miss Brontë's more proper and natural faculty of creative imagination was exempt from its own special chances of error, its own peculiar liabilities to wrong. But from any such error and from any such collapse as those on which we have remarked in others—from all such disloyalty to clear moral law, from all such debasement or degradation of high personal instinct—from all malevolence, from all brutality, from all selfish and vindictive cowardice—from any taint of vile or vulgar or ignoble sympathies, no human spirit was ever more triumphantly delivered—was ever more gloriously free.

Another not insignificant point of difference, though less notable than this, we find in the broad sharp contrast offered by the singular perfection of George Eliot's earliest imaginative work, with its gracious union of ease and strength, its fullness and purity of outline, its clearness and accuracy of touch, its wise and tender equity, its radiant and temperate humour, its harmony and sincerity of tone, to the doubtful, heavy-gaited, floundering tread of Charlotte Brontë's immature and tentative genius, at its first start on the road to so triumphal a goal as lay ahead of it. No reader of average capacity could so far have failed to appreciate the delicate and subtle strength of hand put forth in the 'Scenes of Clerical Life' as to feel any wonder mingling with his sense of admiration when the same fine and potent hand had gathered its latter laurels in a wider field of work; but even the wise and cordial judgment which had discerned the note of power and sincerity perceptible in the crude coarse outlines of 'The Professor' may well have been startled and shaken out of all judicial balance and critical reserve at sight of the sudden sunrise which followed so fast on that diffident uncertain dawn. One of the two only women among their contemporaries, who for absolute inspiration of positive genius may without absurdity of anticlimax be named beside Charlotte Brontë and her sister, has told how sudden and how perfect was the conversion wrought by a first reading of the manuscript of 'Indiana' on the grim and truculent amity of her first literary tutor and censor, the Rhadamanthine author of 'Fragoletta'; who certainly, to judge by his own examples of construction, had some right to pronounce with authority how a novel ought *not* to be written. But the transfiguration of spirit and power revealed by the marvellous advent of the English masterpiece has in it a more splendid sign of miracle than the fiery daybreak of George Sand's.

There is yet a third point of contrast which could not be passed over without such gross and grievous injustice to the very loveliest quality of George Eliot's work as might deservedly expose me to the disgraceful danger of a niche in the temple of ill-fame by the side of those reserved for the representative successors of Messrs. Gifford and Croker. No man or woman, as far as I can recollect, outside the order of poets, has ever written of children with such adorable fidelity of affection as the spiritual mother of Totty, of Eppie, and of Lillo. The fiery-hearted Vestal of Haworth had no room reserved in the palace of her passionate and high-minded imagination as a nursery for inmates of such divine and delicious quality. There is a certain charm of attraction as well as compassion wrought upon us by the tragic childhood of Jane Eyre; and no study can exceed for exquisite veracity and pathos the subtle and faultless portrait of the child Paulina in the opening chapters of 'Villette'; but the attraction of these is not wholly or mainly the charm of infancy, as felt either in actual fleshly life or in simple reflection from the flawless mirror of loving and adoring genius; it comes rather from the latent suggestion or refraction of the woman yet to be,

E

struck sharply back or dimly shaded out from the deep glass held up to us of a passionate and visionary childhood. We begin at once to consider how the children in Charlotte Brontë's books will grow up; it is too evident that they are not there for their own childish sake—a fatal and infallible note of inferiority from the baby-worshipper's point of view. What thickest-headed quarterly section or subdivision of a human dullard ever vexed his pitifully scant quarter of an average allowance of brains with the question how Totty would grow up, and whether or not into a modified likeness of her mother? She is Totty for ever and ever, a doubly immortal little child, set in the lap of our love for the kisses and the laughter of all time, to the last generation of possible human readers. But of Paulina we cannot choose but take thought with Lucy Snowe how such 'a very unique child' will grow up, and what brighter or darker chances may then bring out in full her terrible incalculable capacity of suffering and of love. And, hard though it may be to determine as with legal precision what strange shape and colour may not be taken by human affections under the pressure of circumstance or the strain of suffering, it is yet so difficult to believe, for instance, in the dread and repulsion felt by a forsaken wife and tortured mother for the very beauty and dainty sweetness of her only new-born child, as recalling the cruel sleek charm of the human tiger who had begotten it, that we are wellnigh moved to think one of the most powerfully and exquisitely written chapters in 'Shirley' a chapter which could hardly have been written at all by a woman, or for that matter by a man, of however kindly and noble a nature, in whom the instinct or nerve or organ of love for children was even of average natural strength and sensibility. Milton might have conceived such a thing, but certainly not Shakespeare ; or Corneille, but assuredly not Hugo. Motherhood to Charlotte Brontë must have been a more vague and dim abstraction than his camel to the mythical sage of Germany or his seaport to the nautical king of Bohemia. In George Eliot it is the most vivid and vital impulse which lends to her large intelligence the utmost it ever has of the spiritual breath and living blood of genius; and never had any such a gift more plainly and immediately as from the very heart of heaven.

Most of her men may have been overpraised by her blatant and loose-tongued outriders or pursuivants in the world of letters; and some also of her women may have been praised at least up to the mark of their deserts; not one of her little children even can be. They are good enough to play with the little people of the greatest among poets, from Astyanax down to Mamillius, and onwards again even to that poor 'Petit Paul' but now baptized as in the tears—'tears such as angels weep'—of our mighty and most loving Master. None among the many and truly great qualities of their illustrious mother seems to me so precious as this one; so wholly worthy of the more tender tribute paid by men's loving thanks to something other if not lovelier, and sweeter if less rare, than genius.

But saving for her 'plentiful lack' of inborn baby-worship I cannot think of any great good quality most proper to the most noble among women which was not eminent in the genius as in the nature of Charlotte Brontë. Take for example neither of her great two masterpieces, but the most unequal and least fortunate of her three great books. Weakest on that very side where the others are strongest, 'Shirley' is doubtless a notable example of failure in the central and crucial point of masculine character. Robert Moore is rather dubious than damnable as a study from the male; but for his brother the most fervent of special pleaders can hardly find much to say on that score. No quainter example of a woman of genius in breeches—and very badly fashioned and badly fitting breeches too—was ever exhibited by George Sand's very self, in the days when she refused or accorded the gift of a memorial button off her own to the soft petition of the suppliant Heine. Assuredly 'Louis Moore' would never have passed muster with the very stolidest of all Swiss as the one unmistakable young man in a masquerading party of questionably mingled sexes—as I suppose we are bound to take her word for it that the author of 'Lettres d'un Voyageur' did actually succeed in passing. Glorious words are given him to utter, but they come as from under a mask without eyesight or feature or native organ of speech. Miss Brontë has written nothing finer, nothing of more vivid and exquisite eloquence, than the best passages of his diary; than the sweet and sublime rhapsody on a

windy moonlit vigil, where the words have in them the very breath and magic and riotous radiance, the utter rapture and passion and splendour of the high sonorous night. No other woman that I know of, not George Sand herself, could have written a prose sentence of such exalted and perfect poetry as this:—
'The moon reigns glorious, glad of the gale; as glad as if she gave herself to its fierce caress with love.' Nothing can beat that; no one can match it: it is the first and last absolute and sufficient and triumphant word ever to be said on the subject. It paints wind like David Cox, and light like Turner. To find anything like it in verse we must go to the highest springs of all; to Pindar or to Shelley or to Hugo. And these, in the famous phrase of Brummell's valet—these are her failures.

But what shall be said of her successes? Let us again take a single instance in witness of what one woman, and one only in all time, has done for proof of what the greatest of her kind can do in the loftiest way of moral insight and dramatic imagination. Cervantes alone among all men has done the like; for Sterne has not; for Thackeray has not. There is no first sense of weakness or faultiness or moral grotesque on his part, of pity or question or amusement but half compatible with reverence and tender respect on our own, to overcome in the case of Uncle Toby; if from the first we have to smile at him, we never from the first have to wince or start as at something incongruous with the qualities which evoke our general and affectionate regard. And in the case of

Colonel Newcome our sense of his intellectual infirmity and imperfection is never quite overcome or transfigured by our sense of his moral and chivalrous excellence; if indeed it will ever quite allow us to shake or drive off the lurking or recurring impression that in the author's mind the very idea of goodness was inseparably inwoven and inwound with the thought of some qualifying deformity or characteristic debility, of something in the very essence of its composition inferior and infirm; some weakness or malformation of mind, some sprawling or splay-footed imbecility corresponding to the physical disfigurement of Major Dobbin. One reason or explanation not visibly inapt or inadequate to account for this ungracious impression and the inevitable discomfort or disrelish left by it on the reader's taste may perhaps be found to lie in the curiously undisguised and exuberant admiration with which his creator dilates and expatiates on the charm and perfection of the good Colonel's unquestionable goodness; displaying as it were with insistent ostentation a frankness of sympathy and irrepressible effusion of demonstrative esteem for magnanimity and virtue, which in time of afterthought may or may not make us like all the better and respect all the more the personality and manhood of the workman, but which in either case must needs to some extent impair rather than enhance the actual and present impression of his work.

For the creator of Don Quixote we need make no such allowance; we need make no such reservation on her behalf whose crowning title to men's honour is that she was the creator of Paul Emanuel. Had she none other than this only, yet this alone would place her among the highest of human rulers in ' the brightest heaven of invention '—

λαμπροὺς δυνάστας ἐμπρέποντας αἰθέρι.

Most children, I suppose, who are at once given to dreaming and capable of devotion, must know the mood of loyal fancy and tender ardour so perfectly expressed in the wish of Mrs. Gaskell's little Maggie that she could have waited as a servant on Don Quixote; and the feeling is akin to this with which at a later age any one of kindred nature, on their first intimate acquaintance, and in a great degree ever after, is certain to regard M. Paul. Supreme as is the spiritual triumph of Cervantes in the person of his perfect knight over all insult and mockery of brutal chance and ruffianly realities, all cudgels and all cheats and all contumely, it is hardly a more marvellous or a completer example of imaginative and moral mastery than the triumph of Charlotte Brontë in the quaint person of her grim little Professor over his own eccentric infirmities of habit and temper, more hazardous to our sense of respect than any outward risk or infliction of alien violence or mockery from duchesses or muleteers; a triumph so naturally drawn out and delicately displayed in the swift steady gradations of change and development, now ludicrous and now attractive, and wellnigh adorable at last, through which the figure of M. Paul seems to pass as under summer lights and shadows, till it gradually opens upon us in human fullness of self-unconscious charm and almost sacred beauty—yet always with the sense of some latent infusion, some tender native admixture of a quality at once loveable and laughable; with something indeed of that quaint sweet kind of earnest affection and half-smiling veneration which all men fit to read him feel to their 'heart's root' for the person even more than for the writings of Charles Lamb. That our smile should in no wise impair for one instant our reverence, that our reverence should in no wise make us abashed or ashamed for one moment at the recollection of our smile—this is the final test and triumph of a genius to which we find no likeness outside the very highest rank of creators in the sphere of spiritual invention or of moral imagination.

All who have ever read it will remember the exquisite saying of Chateaubriand so exquisitely rendered by Mr. Arnold :—' The true tears are those which are called forth by the beauty of poetry ; there must be as much admiration in them as sorrow.' The true tears are also those of a yet rarer kind, which are called up at least, if not called forth, by the beauty of goodness ; and in such unshed tears as these are the thoughts as it were baptised, which attend upon our memory of some few among the imperishable shadows of men created by man's genius ; phantoms more actual and vital than the creators they outlive, as mankind outlives the gods of its own creation. There is or should be for all men such consecration in a great man's tears as cannot but glorify the source and embalm the subject of their flow. We may even, and not unreasonably, suspect and fear that it must be through some defect or default in ourselves if we cannot feel as they do the force or charm of that which touches others, and these our betters as often as our equals, so nearly; if we cannot, for example,—as I may regretfully confess that I never could— feel adequately or in full the bitter sweetness that so many thousands—and most notably among them all a better man by far and a far worthier judge than I—have tasted in those pages of Dickens which hold the story of Little Nell; a story in which all the elaborate accumulation of pathetic incident and interest, so tenderly and studiously built up, has never, to speak truth, given me one passing thrill—in the exquisitely fit and faithful phrase of a great living poet, one 'sweet possessive pang'—of the tender delight and pity requickened wellnigh to tears at every fresh reperusal or chance recollection of that one simpler page in 'Bleak House' which describes the baby household tended by the little sister who leaves her lesser charges locked up while she goes out charing; a page which I can imagine that many a man unused to the melting mood would not undertake to read out aloud without a break. But this inability to feel with those who have been most deeply moved by the earlier design of the same great master—sovereign over all

F

competitors of his country and his day in the conterminous provinces of laughter and of tears—this incompetence or obduracy of temper is anything but a source of self-complacent satisfaction when I remember that foremost among these was the illustrious man of lion-hearted genius who but thirteen years since was still our greatest countryman surviving from an age of godlike giants and gods as yet but half divine; the Roman who best knew Greece, the Englishman who best loved England; the friend of Pericles and of Chatham, the associate of Sophocles and of Shakespeare; the heroic poet who retained at the age of Nestor whatever qualities were noblest in the nature of Achilles—all the lightnings of his mortal wrath, and all the tenderness of his immortal tears.

It is certainly no subject for a boast—perhaps it properly should rather be matter for a blush—that Landor's little favourite among all the deathless children begotten by the genius of Dickens should never have had power to work such transformation on my eyes as many a line of his own in verse or prose has wrought so many a time upon them: for if ever that sovereign power of perfection was made manifest in human words, such words assuredly were his, whether English or Latin, who wrote that epitaph on the martyred patriots of Spain, as far exceeding in its majesty of beauty the famous inscription for the Spartan three hundred as the law of the love of liberty exceeds all human laws of mere obedience; who gave back Iphigenia to Agamemnon for ever, and Vipsania for an hour to Tiberius. Before the breath of such a spirit as speaks in his transcendent words, the spirit of a loyal-minded man is bowed down as it were at a touch and melted into burning tears, to be again raised up by it and filled and kindled and expanded into something—or he dreams so—of a likeness for the moment to itself.

Some portion of a faculty such as this, some touch of the same godlike and wonder-working might of imperious moral quality, some flush of the same divine and plenary inspiration, there was likewise in the noble genius and heroic instinct of Charlotte Brontë. Some part of the power denied to many a writer of more keen and rare intelligence than even hers we feel 'to the finest fibre of our nature' at the slight strong touch of her magnetic hand. The phrase of 'passionate perfection,' devised by Mr. Tennyson to describe the rarest type of highest human character, is admirably applicable to her special style at its best. The figure of the young missionary St. John Rivers is by no means to be rated as one of her great unsurpassable successes in spiritual portraiture; the central mainspring of his hard fanatic heroism is never quite adequately touched; her own apparent lack of sympathy with this white marble clergyman (counterpart, as it were, of the 'black marble' Brocklehurst, who chills and darkens the dreary dawn of the story) seems here and there as though it scarcely could be held down by force of artistic conscience from passing into actual and avowed aversion; but the imperishable passion and perfection of the words describing the moorland scene of which his eyes at parting take their long last look must have drawn the tears to many another man's that his own were not soft enough to shed.

This instinct (if I may so call it) for the tragic use of landscape was wellnigh even more potent and conspicuous in Emily than in Charlotte. Little need was there for the survivor to tell us in such earnest and tender words of memorial record how 'my sister Emily loved the moors': that love exhales, as a fresh wild odour from a bleak shrewd soil, from every storm-swept page of 'Wuthering Heights.' All the heart of the league-long billows of rolling and breathing and brightening heather is blown with the breath of it on our faces as we read; all the wind and all the sound and all the fragrance and freedom and gloom and glory of the high north moorland—'in winter nothing more dreary, in summer nothing more divine.' Even in Charlotte Brontë's highest work I find no touches of such exquisite strength and triumphant simplicity as here. There is nothing known to me in any book of quite equal or similar effect to that conveyed by one or two of these. Take for instance that marvellous note of landscape struck as it seems unconsciously by the heaven-born instinct of a supreme artist in composition and colour, in tones and shades and minor notes of tragic and magic sweetness, which serves as overture to the last fierce rapturous passage of raging love and mad recrimination between Heathcliff and the dying Catherine; the mention of the church-bell that in winter could just be heard ringing right across the naked little glen, but in summer the sound was lost, muffled by the murmur of blowing foliage and branches full of birds. The one thing I know or can remember as in some sort comparable in its effect to this passage is of course that notice of the temple-haunting martlet and its loved mansionry which serves as prelude to the entrance of Lady Macbeth from under the buttresses where its pendant bed and procreant cradle bore witness to the delicate air in which incarnate murder also was now to breed and haunt. Even more wonderful perhaps in serene perfection of subdued and sovereign power is the last brief paragraph of that stormy and fiery tale. There was a dark unconscious instinct as of primitive nature-worship in the passionate great genius of Emily Brontë, which found no corresponding quality in her sister's. It is into the lips of her representative Shirley Keeldar that Charlotte puts the fervent 'pagan' hymn of visionary praise to her mother nature—Hertha, Demeter, 'la déesse des dieux,' which follows on her fearless indignant repudiation of Milton and his Eve. Nor had Charlotte's less old-world and Titanic soul any touch of the self-dependent solitary contempt for all outward objects of faith and hope, for all aspiration after a changed heart or a contrite spirit or a converted mind, which speaks in the plain-song note of Emily's clear stern verse with such grandeur of antichristian fortitude and self-controlling self-reliance, that the 'halting slave' of Epaphroditus might have owned for his spiritual sister the English girl whose only prayer for herself, ' in life and death'—a self-sufficing prayer, self-answered, and fulfilled even in the utterance—was for 'a chainless soul, with courage to endure.' Not often probably has such a petition gone up from within the walls of a country parsonage as this :—

> And if I pray, the only prayer
> That moves my lips for me,
> Is—Leave the heart that now I bear,
> And give me liberty!

That word which is above every word might surely have been found written on that heart. Her love of earth for earth's sake, her tender loyalty and passionate reverence for the All-mother, bring to mind the words of her sister's friend, and the first eloquent champion of her own genius:—

> I praise thee, mother earth! oh earth, my mother!
> Oh earth, sweet mother! gentle mother earth!
> Whence thou receivest what thou givest I
> Ask not as a child asketh not his mother,
> Oh earth, my mother!

No other poet's imagination could have conceived that agony of the girl who dreams she is in heaven, and weeps so bitterly for the loss of earth that the angels cast her out in anger, and she finds herself fallen on the moss and heather of the mid moor-head, and wakes herself with sobbing for joy. It is possible that to take full delight in Emily Brontë's book one must have something by natural inheritance of her instinct and something by earliest association of her

love for the same special points of earth—
the same lights and sounds and colours
and odours and sights and shapes of the
same fierce free landscape of tenantless and
fruitless and fenceless moor; but however
that may be, it was assuredly with no less
justice of insight and accuracy of judgment
than humility of self-knowledge and fidelity of love that Charlotte in her day of
solitary fame assigned to her dead sister
the crown of poetic honour which she as
rightfully disclaimed for herself. Full of
poetic quality as her own work is throughout, that quality is never condensed or
crystallised into the proper and final form
of verse. But the pure note of absolutely
right expression for things inexpressible in
full by prose at its highest point of ade-

quacy—the formal inspiration of sound which at once reveals itself, and which can fully reveal itself by metrical embodiment alone, in the symphonies and antiphonies of regular word-music and definite instinctive modulation of corresponsive tones—this is what Emily had for her birthright as certainly as Charlotte had it not. Here are a few lines to give evidence for themselves on that score.

> He comes with western winds, with evening's wandering airs,
> With that clear dusk of heaven that brings the thickest stars.
> Winds take a pensive tone, and stars a tender fire,
> And visions rise, and change, that kill me with desire.
>
> Desire for nothing known in my maturer years,
> When Joy grew mad with awe, at counting future tears.
> * * * * * *
> Oh, dreadful is the check—intense the agony—
> When the ear begins to hear, and the eye begins to see;
> When the pulse begins to throb, the brain to think again,
> The soul to feel the flesh, and the flesh to feel the chain.

If here is not the pure distinctive note of song as opposed to speech—the 'lyrical cry,' as Mr. Arnold calls it—I know not where to seek it in English verse since Shelley. Another such unmistakable note is struck in the verses headed 'Remembrance,' where the deep sense of division wellnigh melts and dies into a dream of reunion and revival by the might of memories 'that are most dearly sweet and bitter.' Here too is the same profound perception of an abiding power, but little less if surely less than omnipotence, in the old dumb divinities of Earth and Time—gods only not yet found strong enough to divide long love from death;

> Severed at last by Time's all-severing wave.

All these samples are from the little

triune publication of 1846; which gave also some witness of the latent and labouring powers, as yet unsure of aim and outlet, but feeling their unquiet way to right and left in the deep underworld of Charlotte Brontë's growing genius. But the final expression in verse of Emily's passionate and inspired intelligence was to be uttered from lips already whitened though not yet chilled by the present shadow of unterrifying death. No last words of poet or hero or sage or saint were ever worthy of longer and more reverent remembrance than that appeal which is so far above and beyond a prayer to the indestructible God within herself; a psalm of trust so strangely (as it seems) compounded of personal and pantheistic faith, at once fiery and solemn, full alike of resignation and of rapture, far alike from the conventions of vulgar piety and the complacencies of scientific limitation; as utterly disdainful of doctrine as of doubt, as contemptuous of hearsay as reverent of itself, as wholly stripped and cleared and lightened from all burdens and all bandages and all incrustations of creed as it is utterly pervaded and possessed by the sublime and irrefutable passion of belief.

The praise of Emily Brontë can be no alien or discursive episode in the briefest and most cursory notice, the least adequate or exhaustive panegyric of her sister; and far less would it have seemed less than indispensable to that most faithful and devoted spirit of indomitable love which kept such constant watch over her memory, and fought so good a fight for her fame. There is no more significant or memorable touch of nature in the records of her noble soul and unalterable heart than we find in her instant and her lifelong thankfulness for the fervent tribute of Mr. Dobell to the profound and subtle genius, then already fallen still and silent, which had moved as a wind upon the tragic and perilous waters of passion overtopped by the shadow of 'Wuthering Heights.' Those who would understand Charlotte, even more than those who would understand Emily, should study the difference of tenderness between the touch that drew Shirley Keeldar and the touch that drew Lucy Snowe. This latter figure, as Mr. Wemyss Reid has observed with indisputable accuracy of insight, was doubtless, if never meant to win liking or made to find favour in the general reader's eyes, yet none the less evidently on that account the faithful likeness of Charlotte Brontë, studied from the life, and painted by her own hand with the sharp austere precision of a photograph rather than a portrait. But it is herself with the consolation and support of her genius withdrawn, with the strength of her spiritual arm immeasurably shortened, the cunning of her right hand comparatively cancelled; and this it is that makes the main undertone and ultimate result of the book somewhat mournfuller even than the literal record of her mournful and glorious life. In the house where I now write this there is a picture which I have known through all the years I can remember—a landscape by Crome;

showing just a wild sad track of shoreward brushwood and chill fen, blasted and wasted by the bitter breath of the east wind blowing off the eastward sea, shrivelled and subdued and resigned as it were with a sort of grim submission to the dumb dark tyranny of a full-charged thunder-cloud which masks the mid heaven of midnoon with the heavy muffler of midnight, and leaves but here and there a dull fierce gleam of discomfortable and deadened sunlight along the haggard sky-line or below it. As with all this it is yet always a pleasure to look upon so beautiful and noble a study of so sad and harsh-featured an outlying byway through the weariest waste places of the world, so is it in its kind a perpetual pleasure to revisit the wellnigh sunless landscape of Lucy Snowe's sad, passionate, and valiant life. But to us, knowing what we all now know of the designer, there seems a touch of pathos beyond all articulate expression in the contrast, when we turn from this to the ideal decoration of Shirley Keeldar's, and remember that here is the vision of the life she would fain have realized for her dead and best beloved and most dearly honoured sister; who had had in the days of her actual life as harsh and strange a time of it as her own. From the character of Shirley, as from the character of Lucy Snowe, the artist has naturally as of necessity withdrawn the component element that in its effect and result at least was or is for us now the dominant and distinctive quality of Emily Brontë as of Charlotte—the special gift and application of her creative genius; and on the other hand we can barely imagine that austere and fiery poetess, a creature so admirably and terribly compounded of tragic genius and Stoic heroism, a jester of pleasantry so bitter and so grim in those brief bleak flashes of northern humour that lighten across the byways of her book from the rigid old lips of the Calvinist farm-servant —we can barely, I say, conceive of her as exchanging such rapid passes of light bright fence in a laughing war of words with the reverend and gallant old Cossack Helstone as sharpen and quicken the dialogue and action of the most gracious and joyous interlude in 'Shirley.' Yet surely Charlotte should have known as well as she loved her sister; and therefore we may more reasonably and more confidently infer that but for the brilliant study of Shirley Keeldar we should never have seen with the eye of our imagination any other than a misconceived and mutilated portrait, a disfigured and discoloured likeness of Emily Brontë; one curtailed of the fair proportions, if not diminished from the natural stature of her spirit; discrowned and disinherited of its livelier and gentler charm of living feature, though not degraded or dethroned from the august succession to their strength for endurance or rebellion most beseeming a lineal daughter of the earth-born giants, more ancient in their godlike lineage than all modern reigning gods.

The habit of direct study from life which has given us, among its finest and most precious results, these two contrasted figures of

Shirley Keeldar and Lucy Snowe, affords yet another point of contrast or distinction between the manner and motive of work respectively perceptible in the design of either sister. Emily Brontë, like William Blake, would probably have said, or at least would presumably have felt, that such study after the model was to her impossible—an attempt but too certain to diminish her imaginative insight and disable her creative hand; while Charlotte evidently never worked so well as when painting more or less directly from nature. Almost the only apparent exception, as far as we—the run of her readers—know, is the wonderful and incomparable figure of Rochester. For M. Paul she must have had some kind of model, however transfigured and dilated by the splendid influence of her own genius; for such studies as Madame Beck and Miss Fanshawe she doubtless had the sitters in her mind's eye as clearly and as close as under the lens of a photographic machine; but how she came first to conceive and finally to fashion that perfect study of noble and faultful and suffering manhood remains one of the most insoluble riddles ever set by genius as a snare or planned as a maze for the judgment of any lesser intelligence than its own. There in any case is the result— alive at all events, and deathless; defiant alike of explanation or reproduction by any critic or copyist. The incredible absurdity and the ineffable impertinence of one solution proposed at the time, which sought in the dedication of the book for a hint at the original of the hero, were worthy of the flatheaded and fork-tongued generation which could produce a notorious comment on 'Jane Eyre,' to the effect that its author must be a woman who long since had deservedly forfeited the society of her own sex. It is of infinitely small moment that we know only by its offence the obscene animal now nailed up for this offence by the ear, though not by name—its particular name being as undiscoverable as its generic designation is unmistakable—to the undecaying gibbet of immemorial contempt. When a farmer used to nail a dead polecat on the outside of his barndoor, it was surely less from any specific personal rancour of retaliatory animosity towards that particular creature than by way of judicial admonition to the tribe as yet untrapped, the horde as yet unhanged, which might survive to lament, if not to succeed, the malodorous malefactor. No mortal can now be curious to verify the name as well as the nature of the typical specimen which then emitted in one spasm of sub-human spite at once the snarl and the stench proper to its place and kind. But we know that from the earlier days of Shelley onwards to these later days of Tennyson, whatsoever things are true, whatsoever things are honest, whatsoever things are just, whatsoever things are pure, whatsoever things are lovely, whatsoever things are of good report, become untrue, dishonest, unjust, impure, unlovely, and ill-famed, when passed through the critical crucible of the Quarterly Review.

For many among the minor types in

Charlotte Brontë's works it was seemingly somewhat easier than perhaps it should have been at the time of their appearance to detect the living and not always other than unoffending antitypes. If the immortal three curates of 'Shirley' did indeed admit their respective likenesses, and accept for each other and themselves the names by which they were rebaptized in such bitter waters of ridicule—a font filled rather from the springs of Marah than the stream of Jordan, which served Chateaubriand's purpose so much better than the upshot of the ceremony would seem to have served his prince—it must in common justice be owned that the admirable candour and good humour of her models should have touched their satirist with a sense of something keener than compunction; for such simple honesty and hearty courtesy as must have been more than needed to make the very dullest and most impervious of reverend or irreverend gentlemen continue to bear themselves with the frank civility of kindly custom towards the solitary and sorrowful woman whose scornful genius had done its worst on them—and that worst, even to a thick-headed and thick-skinned victim, how terrible!—must surely also have been more than sufficient to disprove the full justice of the caricature, and impeach the accuracy of whatever was most offensive in her design or injurious in her imputations. To the vivid yet temperate fidelity of the Yorke family group we have the witness of a member offered to the photographer of that singular and sharply outlined circle. In most cases probably the design begun by means of the camera was transferred for completion to the canvass. The likeness of Mr. Helstone to Mr. Brontë, for example, was thus at once enlarged and subdued, heightened and modified, by the skilful and noble instinct which kept it always within the gracious and natural bounds prescribed and maintained by the fine tact of filial respect. No more lifelike or memorable portrait was ever wrought into the composition of an ideal or historic picture by the loftiest art of any Venetian painter. The man's hard, rigid, contemptuous, yet never quite unkindly or unrighteous force of character—his keen enjoyment of action and struggle, his fierce imperious relish of resistance—the fine soldierly quality of spirit, somewhat too generally mistimed or misplaced, for lack of fit or full occasion to call it forth, which makes him always less ready to 'go with sir priest than sir knight'—all these points are relieved and combined with a skill and strength of touch, perhaps incomparable in the work of any other woman.

But time and cunning would fail us to discover, as art and eloquence would fail us to commend, a tithe of the examples that might and should be cited in evidence of that noble and fruitful genius which found in the frail temple of her mortal life a minister so high and pure of spirit, so faithful and heroic of heart. Nowhere is its peculiar gift of subtle and pathetic veracity more notable than in the brief last pages written between the too closely neighbouring dates of her marriage and her death ; a precious fragment to which the few and fine words of introduction prefixed by the illustrious writer who had been the peculiar god of her inmost idolatry have always seemed to me worthy of special remembrance among the truest and the noblest, the manliest and the kindliest lines that ever came from the pen of Mr. Thackeray. It is a coincidence as memorable as it is deplorable that so many of the best and greatest who have died within the reach of our recollection should have left, like these, some splendid and broken sample of their highest workmanship unfinished for the admiration and the craving and the fruitless passionate regret of aftertime ; even as Shakespeare himself left behind him the two colossal fragments that a hand in the one case only lesser than his own, in the other case as impotent and impertinent as the hand of his very worst and latest commentator, ventured to rehandle and recast into the shapes under which we know them as 'Timon of Athens' and 'The Two Noble Kinsmen.' Too soon after he had 'taken to foster' Charlotte Brontë's little orphan tale of 'Emma,' Mr. Thackeray had in turn to leave half unshapen, and recognisable only by grand rough indications of its giant parentage, what should have been the stateliest and most stalwart offspring of his latter years—born to disprove the premature charge of comparative decadence and debility not unjustly incurred by its more immediate predecessors; then the great man so improperly rated as his rival passed also away in the mid heat of work, leaving again but a bright fragment of perplexing shape and splendour; and now but lately the biographer of Dickens likewise has left us cheated of the ardent and grateful hopes that were fixed on the completion of the first adequate or trustworthy Life of Swift. Not one of these nor of all their generation has left or yet will leave a nobler memory, and it may well be that in the eyes of Englishmen yet unborn not one will be found to have left a nobler memorial, than the unforgotten life and the imperishable works of Charlotte Brontë.

THE END.

[April, 1885.

CHATTO & WINDUS'S
LIST OF BOOKS.

* * * * * * * * * * * *

About.—The Fellah: An Egyptian Novel. By EDMOND ABOUT. Translated by Sir RANDAL ROBERTS. Post 8vo, illustrated boards, 2s.; cloth limp, 2s. 6d.

Adams (W. Davenport), Works by:
A Dictionary of the Drama. Being a comprehensive Guide to the Plays, Playwrights, Players, and Playhouses of the United Kingdom and America, from the Earliest to the Present Times. Crown 8vo, half-bound, 12s. 6d. [*Preparing.*
Latter-Day Lyrics. Edited by W. DAVENPORT ADAMS. Post 8vo, cloth limp, 2s. 6d.
Quips and Quiddities. Selected by W. DAVENPORT ADAMS. Post 8vo, cloth limp, 2s. 6d.

Advertising, A History of, from the Earliest Times. Illustrated by Anecdotes, Curious Specimens, and Notices of Successful Advertisers. By HENRY SAMPSON. Crown 8vo, with Coloured Frontispiece and Illustrations, cloth gilt, 7s. 6d.

Agony Column (The) of "The Times," from 1800 to 1870. Edited, with an Introduction, by ALICE CLAY. Post 8vo, cloth limp, 2s. 6d.

Aide (Hamilton), Works by:
Carr of Carrlyon. Post 8vo, illustrated boards, 2s.
Confidences. Post 8vo, illustrated boards, 2s.

Alexander (Mrs.) NOVELS by:
Post 8vo, illustrated boards, 2s.; crown 8vo, cloth extra, 3s. 6d. each.
Maid, Wife, or Widow? A Romance.
Valerie's Fate.

Allen (Grant), Works by:
Crown 8vo, cloth extra, 6s. each.
The Evolutionist at Large. Second Edition, revised.
Vignettes from Nature.
Colin Clout's Calendar.
Strange Stories. With a Frontispiece by GEORGE DU MAURIER.

Architectural Styles, A Handbook of. Translated from the German of A. ROSENGARTEN, by W. COLLETT-SANDARS. Crown 8vo, cloth extra, with 639 Illustrations, 7s. 6d.

Art (The) of Amusing: A Collection of Graceful Arts, Games, Tricks, Puzzles, and Charades. By FRANK BELLEW. With 300 Illustrations. Cr. 8vo, cloth extra, 4s. 6d.

Artemus Ward:
Artemus Ward's Works: The Works of CHARLES FARRER BROWNE, better known as ARTEMUS WARD. With Portrait and Facsimile. Crown 8vo, cloth extra, 7s. 6d.
Artemus Ward's Lecture on the Mormons. With 32 Illustrations Edited, with Preface, by EDWARD P. HINGSTON. Crown 8vo, 6d.
The Genial Showman: Life and Adventures of Artemus Ward. By EDWARD P. HINGSTON. With a Frontispiece. Cr. 8vo, cl. extra, 3s. 6d.

Ashton (John), Works by:
A History of the Chap-Books of the Eighteenth Century. With nearly 400 Illusts., engraved in facsimile of the originals. Cr. 8vo, cl. ex., 7s. 6d.
Social Life in the Reign of Queen Anne. From Original Sources. With nearly 100 Illusts. Cr.8vo,cl.ex.,7s.6d.
Humour, Wit, and Satire of the Seventeenth Century. With nearly 100 Illusts. Cr. 8vo, cl. extra, 7s. 6d.
English Caricature and Satire on Napoleon the First. 120 Illusts. from Originals. Two Vols., demy 8vo, 28s.

Bacteria.—A Synopsis of the Bacteria and Yeast Fungi and Allied Species. By W. B. GROVE, B.A. With 87 Illusts. Crown 8vo, cl. extra, 3s. 6d.

Balzac's "Comedie Humaine" and its Author. With Translations by H. H. WALKER. Post 8vo, cl. limp, 2s. 6d.

Bankers, A Handbook of London; together with Lists of Bankers from 1677. By F. G. HILTON PRICE. Crown 8vo, cloth extra, 7s. 6d.

Bardsley (Rev. C.W.), Works by:
English Surnames: Their Sources and Significations. Third Ed., revised. Cr. 8vo, cl. extra, 7s. 6d.
Curiosities of Puritan Nomenclature. Crown 8vo, cloth extra, 7s. 6d.

Bartholomew Fair, Memoirs of. By HENRY MORLEY. With 100 Illusts. Crown 8vo, cloth extra, 7s. 6d.

Basil, Novels by:
A Drawn Game. Cr. 8vo., cl. ex., 3s. 6d.
The Wearing of the Green. Three Vols., crown 8vo, 31s. 6d.

Beaconsfield, Lord: A Biography. By T. P. O'CONNOR, M.P. Sixth Edit., New Preface. Cr.8vo,cl.ex.7s.6d.

Beauchamp. — Grantley Grange: A Novel. By SHELSLEY BEAUCHAMP. Post 8vo, illust. bds., 2s.

Beautiful Pictures by British Artists: A Gathering of Favourites from our Picture Galleries. In Two Series. All engraved on Steel in the highest style of Art. Edited, with Notices of the Artists, by SYDNEY ARMYTAGE, M.A. Imperial 4to, cloth extra, gilt and gilt edges, 21s. per Vol.

Bechstein.—As Pretty as Seven, and other German Stories. Collected by LUDWIG BECHSTEIN. With Additional Tales by the Brothers GRIMM, and 100 Illusts. by RICHTER. Small 4to, green and gold, 6s. 6d.; gilt edges, 7s. 6d.

Beerbohm.—Wanderings in Patagonia; or, Life among the Ostrich Hunters. By JULIUS BEERBOHM. With Illusts. Crown 8vo, cloth extra, 3s. 6d.

Belgravia for 1885. One Shilling Monthly, Illustrated by P. MACNAB.—A Strange Voyage, by W. CLARK RUSSELL, is begun in the JANUARY Number, and will be continued throughout the year. This Number contains also the Opening Chapters of a New Story by CECIL POWER, Author of "Philistia," entitled Babylon.
*** *Now ready, the Volume for* NOVEMBER, 1884, *to* FEBRUARY, 1885, *cloth extra, gilt edges,* 7s. 6d.; *Cases for binding Vols.,* 2s. *each.*

Belgravia Holiday Number. With Stories by F. W. ROBINSON, JUSTIN H. MCCARTHY, B. MONTGOMERIE RANKING, and others. Demy 8vo, with Illusts., 1s. [*July.*

Bennett (W.C.,LL.D.),Works by:
A Ballad History of England. Post 8vo, cloth limp, 2s.
Songs for Sailors. Post 8vo, cloth limp, 2s.

Besant (Walter) and James Rice, Novels by. Post 8vo, illust. boards, 2s. each; cloth limp, 2s. 6d. each; or cr. 8vo, cl. extra, 3s. 6d. each.
Ready-Money Mortiboy.
With Harp and Crown.
This Son of Vulcan.
My Little Girl.
The Case of Mr. Lucraft.
The Golden Butterfly.
By Celia's Arbour.
The Monks of Thelema.
'Twas in Trafalgar's Bay.
The Seamy Side.
The Ten Years' Tenant.
The Chaplain of the Fleet.

Besant (Walter), Novels by:
Crown 8vo, cloth extra, 3s. 6d. each; post 8vo, illust. boards, 2s. each; cloth limp, 2s. 6d. each.
All Sorts and Conditions of Men: An Impossible Story. With Illustrations by FRED. BARNARD.
The Captains' Room, &c. With Frontispiece by E. J. WHEELER.
All in a Garden Fair. With 6 Illusts. by H. FURNISS.

Dorothy Forster. New and Cheaper Edition. With Illustrations by CHAS. GREEN. Cr. 8vo, cloth extra, 3s. 6d.
Uncle Jack, and other Stories. Crown 8vo, cloth extra, 6s.

The Art of Fiction. Demy 8vo, 1s.

Betham-Edwards (M.), Novels by. Crown 8vo, cloth extra, 3s. 6d. each.; post 8vo, illust. bds., 2s. each.
Felicia. | Kitty.

Bewick (Thos.) and his Pupils. By AUSTIN DOBSON. With 95 Illustrations. Square 8vo, cloth extra, 10s. 6d.

Birthday Books:—
The Starry Heavens: A Poetical Birthday Book. Square 8vo, handsomely bound in cloth, 2s. 6d.
Birthday Flowers: Their Language and Legends. By W. J. GORDON. Beautifully Illustrated in Colours by VIOLA BOUGHTON. In illuminated cover, crown 4to, 6s.
The Lowell Birthday Book. With Illusts., small 8vo, cloth extra, 4s. 6d.

Blackburn's (Henry) Art Handbooks. Demy 8vo, Illustrated, uniform in size for binding.
Academy Notes, separate years, from 1875 to 1884, each 1s.
Academy Notes, 1885. With numerous Illustrations. 1s.
Academy Notes, 1875-79. Complete in One Vol., with nearly 600 Illusts. in Facsimile. Demy 8vo, cloth limp, 6s.
Academy Notes, 1880-84. Complete in One Volume, with about 700 Facsimile Illustrations. Cloth limp, 6s.
Grosvenor Notes, 1877. 6d.
Grosvenor Notes, separate years, from 1878 to 1884, each 1s.
Grosvenor Notes, 1885. With numerous Illustrations. 1s.
Grosvenor Notes, 1877-82. With upwards of 300 Illustrations. Demy 8vo, cloth limp, 6s.
Pictures at South Kensington. With 70 Illustrations. 1s.
The English Pictures at the National Gallery. 114 Illustrations. 1s.
The Old Masters at the National Gallery. 128 Illustrations. 1s. 6d.
A Complete Illustrated Catalogue to the National Gallery. With Notes by H. BLACKBURN, and 242 Illusts. Demy 8vo, cloth limp, 3s.

Illustrated Catalogue of the Luxembourg Gallery. Containing about 250 Reproductions after the Original Drawings of the Artists. Edited by F. G. DUMAS. Demy 8vo, 3s. 6d.
The Paris Salon, 1884. With over 300 Illusts. Edited by F. G. DUMAS. Demy 8vo, 3s.
The Paris Salon, 1885. With Facsimile Sketches. Edited by F. G. DUMAS. Demy 8vo, 3s.

ART HANDBOOKS, *continued—*
The Art Annual, 1883-4. Edited by F. G. DUMAS. With 300 full-page Illustrations. Demy 8vo, 5s.

Boccaccio's Decameron; or, Ten Days' Entertainment. Translated into English, with an Introduction by THOMAS WRIGHT, F.S.A. With Portrait, and STOTHARD'S beautiful Copperplates. Cr. 8vo, cloth extra, gilt, 7s. 6d.

Blake (William): Etchings from his Works. By W. B. SCOTT. With descriptive Text. Folio, half-bound boards, India Proofs, 21s.

Bowers' (G.) Hunting Sketches:
Canters in Crampshire. Oblong 4to, half-bound boards, 21s.
Leaves from a Hunting Journal Coloured in facsimile of the originals Oblong 4to, half-bound, 21s.

Boyle (Frederick), Works by:
Camp Notes: Stories of Sport and Adventure in Asia, Africa, and America. Crown 8vo, cloth extra 3s. 6d.; post 8vo, illustrated bds., 2s
Savage Life. Crown 8vo, cloth extra 3s. 6d.; post 8vo, illustrated bds., 2s
Chronicles of No-Man's Land Crown 8vo, cloth extra, 6s.; post 8vo, illust. boards, 2s.

Brand's Observations on Popular Antiquities, chiefly Illustrating the Origin of our Vulgar Customs, Ceremonies, and Superstitions. With the Additions of Sir HENRY ELLIS. Crown 8vo, cloth extra, gilt, with numerous Illustrations, 7s. 6d.

Bret Harte, Works by:
Bret Harte's Collected Works. Arranged and Revised by the Author. Complete in Five Vols., crown 8vo, cloth extra, 6s. each.
  Vol. I. COMPLETE POETICAL AND DRAMATIC WORKS. With Steel Portrait, and Introduction by Author.
  Vol. II. EARLIER PAPERS—LUCK OF ROARING CAMP, and other Sketches—BOHEMIAN PAPERS — SPANISH AND AMERICAN LEGENDS.
  Vol. III. TALES OF THE ARGONAUTS—EASTERN SKETCHES.
  Vol. IV. GABRIEL CONROY.
  Vol. V. STORIES — CONDENSED NOVELS, &c.
The Select Works of Bret Harte, in Prose and Poetry. With Introductory Essay by J. M. BELLEW, Portrait of the Author, and 50 Illustrations. Crown 8vo, cloth extra, 7s. 6d.
Gabriel Conroy: A Novel. Post 8vo, illustrated boards, 2s.

BOOKS PUBLISHED BY

Bret **Harte's** Works, *continued*—
- An Heiress of Red Dog, and other Stories. Post 8vo, illustrated boards, 2s.; cloth limp, 2s. 6d.
- The Twins of Table Mountain. Fcap. 8vo, picture cover, 1s.; crown 8vo, cloth extra, 3s. 6d.
- Luck of Roaring Camp, and other Sketches. Post 8vo, illust. bds., 2s.
- Jeff Briggs's Love Story. Fcap. 8vo, picture cover, 1s.; cloth extra, 2s. 6d.
- Flip. Post 8vo, illustrated boards, 2s.; cloth limp, 2s. 6d.
- Californian Stories (including The Twins of Table Mountain, Jeff Briggs's Love Story, &c.) Post 8vo, illustrated boards, 2s.

Brewer (Rev. Dr.), Works by:
- The Reader's Handbook of Allusions, References, Plots, and Stories. Fourth Edition, revised throughout, with a New Appendix, containing a Complete English Bibliography. Cr. 8vo, 1,400 pp., cloth extra, 7s. 6d.
- Authors and their Works, with the Dates: Being the Appendices to "The Reader's Handbook," separately printed. Cr. 8vo, cloth limp, 2s.
- A Dictionary of Miracles: Imitative, Realistic, and Dogmatic. Crown 8vo, cloth extra, 7s. 6d.; half-bound, 9s.

Brewster (Sir David), Works by:
- More Worlds than One: The Creed of the Philosopher and the Hope of the Christian. With Plates. Post 8vo, cloth extra, 4s. 6d.
- The Martyrs of Science: Lives of Galileo, Tycho Brahe, and Kepler. With Portraits. Post 8vo, cloth extra, 4s. 6d.
- Letters on Natural Magic. A New Edition, with numerous Illustrations, and Chapters on the Being and Faculties of Man, and Additional Phenomena of Natural Magic, by J. A. Smith. Post 8vo, cloth extra, 4s. 6d.

Brillat-Savarin.—Gastronomy as a Fine Art. By Brillat-Savarin. Translated by R. E. Anderson, M.A. Post 8vo, cloth limp, 2s. 6d.

Burnett (Mrs.), Novels by:
- Surly Tim, and other Stories. Post 8vo, illustrated boards, 2s.
- Kathleen Mavourneen. Fcap. 8vo, picture cover, 1s.
- Lindsay's Luck. Fcap. 8vo, picture cover, 1s.
- Pretty Polly Pemberton. Fcap. 8vo, picture cover, 1s.

Buchanan's (Robert) Works:
- Ballads of Life, Love, and Humour. With a Frontispiece by Arthur Hughes. Crown 8vo, cloth extra, 6s.
- Selected Poems of Robert Buchanan. With Frontispiece by T. Dalziel. Crown 8vo, cloth extra, 6s.
- Undertones. Cr. 8vo, cloth extra, 6s.
- London Poems. Cr. 8vo, cl. extra, 6s.
- The Book of Orm. Cr. 8vo, cl. ex., 6s.
- White Rose and Red: A Love Story. Crown 8vo, cloth extra, 6s.
- Idylls and Legends of Inverburn. Crown 8vo, cloth extra, 6s.
- St. Abe and his Seven Wives: A Tale of Salt Lake City. With a Frontispiece by A. B. Houghton. Crown 8vo, cloth extra, 5s.
- Robert Buchanan's Complete Poetical Works. With Steel-plate Portrait. Crown 8vo, cloth extra, 7s. 6d.
- The Hebrid Isles: Wanderings in the Land of Lorne and the Outer Hebrides. With Frontispiece by W. Small. Crown 8vo, cloth extra, 6s.
- A Poet's Sketch-Book: Selections from the Prose Writings of Robert Buchanan. Crown 8vo, cl. extra, 6s.
- The Shadow of the Sword: A Romance. Crown 8vo, cloth extra, 3s. 6d.; post 8vo, illust. boards, 2s.
- A Child of Nature: A Romance. With a Frontispiece. Crown 8vo, cloth extra, 3s. 6d.; post 8vo, illust. bds., 2s.
- God and the Man: A Romance. With Illustrations by Fred. Barnard. Crown 8vo, cloth extra, 3s. 6d.; post 8vo, illustrated boards, 2s.
- The Martyrdom of Madeline: A Romance. With Frontispiece by A. W. Cooper. Cr. 8vo, cloth extra, 3s. 6d.; post 8vo, illustrated boards, 2s.
- Love Me for Ever. With a Frontispiece by P. Macnab. Crown 8vo, cloth extra, 3s. 6d.; post 8vo, illustrated boards, 2s.
- Annan Water: A Romance. Crown 8vo, cloth extra, 3s. 6d.; post 8vo, illust. boards, 2s.
- The New Abelard: A Romance. Crown 8vo, cloth extra, 3s. 6d.; post 8vo, illust. boards, 2s.
- Foxglove Manor: A Novel. Crown 8vo, cloth extra, 3s. 6d.
- Matt: A Romance. Crown 8vo, cloth extra, 3s. 6d.

Burton (Robert):
- The Anatomy of Melancholy. A New Edition, complete, corrected and enriched by Translations of the Classical Extracts. Demy 8vo, cloth extra, 7s. 6d.
- Melancholy Anatomised: Being an Abridgment, for popular use, of Burton's Anatomy of Melancholy. Post 8vo, cloth limp, 2s. 6d.

Burton (Captain), Works by:
To the Gold Coast for Gold: A Personal Narrative. By RICHARD F. BURTON and VERNEY LOVETT CAMERON. With Maps and Frontispiece. Two Vols., crown 8vo, cloth extra, 21s.

The Book of the Sword: Being a History of the Sword and its Use in all Countries, from the Earliest Times. By RICHARD F. BURTON. With over 400 Illustrations. Square 8vo, cloth extra, 32s.

Bunyan's Pilgrim's Progress. Edited by Rev. T. SCOTT. With 17 Steel Plates by STOTHARD, engraved by GOODALL, and numerous Woodcuts. Crown 8vo, cloth extra, gilt, 7s. 6d.

Byron (Lord):
Byron's Letters and Journals. With Notices of his Life. By THOMAS MOORE. A Reprint of the Original Edition, newly revised, with Twelve full-page Plates. Crown 8vo, cloth extra, gilt, 7s. 6d.

Byron's Don Juan. Complete in One Vol., post 8vo, cloth limp, 2s.

Cameron (Commander) and Captain Burton.—To the Gold Coast for Gold: A Personal Narrative. By RICHARD F. BURTON and VERNEY LOVETT CAMERON. With Frontispiece and Maps. Two Vols., crown 8vo, cloth extra, 21s.

Cameron (Mrs. H. Lovett), Novels by:
Crown 8vo, cloth extra, 3s. 6d. each; post 8vo, illustrated boards, 2s. each.
Juliet's Guardian.
Deceivers Ever.

Campbell.—White and Black: Travels in the United States. By Sir GEORGE CAMPBELL, M.P. Demy 8vo, cloth extra, 14s.

Carlyle (Thomas):
Thomas Carlyle: Letters and Recollections. By MONCURE D. CONWAY, M.A. Crown 8vo, cloth extra, with Illustrations, 6s.

On the Choice of Books. By THOMAS CARLYLE. With a Life of the Author by R. H. SHEPHERD. New and Revised Edition, post 8vo, cloth extra, Illustrated, 1s. 6d.

The Correspondence of Thomas Carlyle and Ralph Waldo Emerson, 1834 to 1872. Edited by CHARLES ELIOT NORTON. With Portraits. Two Vols., crown 8vo, cloth extra, 24s.

Chapman's (George) Works: Vol. I. contains the Plays complete, including the doubtful ones. Vol. II., the Poems and Minor Translations, with an Introductory Essay by ALGERNON CHARLES SWINBURNE. Vol. III., the Translations of the Iliad and Odyssey. Three Vols., crown 8vo, cloth extra, 18s.; or separately, 6s. each.

Chatto & Jackson.—A Treatise on Wood Engraving, Historical and Practical. By WM. ANDREW CHATTO and JOHN JACKSON. With an Additional Chapter by HENRY G. BOHN; and 450 fine Illustrations. A Reprint of the last Revised Edition. Large 4to, half-bound, 28s.

Chaucer:
Chaucer for Children: A Golden Key. By Mrs. H. R. HAWEIS. With Eight Coloured Pictures and numerous Woodcuts by the Author. New Ed., small 4to, cloth extra, 6s.

Chaucer for Schools. By Mrs. H. R. HAWEIS. Demy 8vo, cloth limp, 2s. 6d.

Clodd — Myths and Dreams. By EDWARD CLODD, F.R.A.S., Author of "The Childhood of Religions," &c. Crown 8vo, cloth extra, 5s.

City (The) of Dream: A Poem. Fcap. 8vo, cloth extra, 6s. [In the press.

Cobban.—The Cure of Souls: A Story. By J. MACLAREN COBBAN. Post 8vo, illustrated boards, 2s.

Collins (C. Allston).—The Bar Sinister: A Story. By C. ALLSTON COLLINS. Post 8vo, illustrated bds., 2s.

Collins (Mortimer & Frances), Novels by:
Sweet and Twenty. Post 8vo, illustrated boards, 2s.
Frances. Post 8vo, illust. bds., 2s.
Blacksmith and Scholar. Post 8vo, illustrated boards, 2s.; crown 8vo, cloth extra, 3s. 6d.
The Village Comedy. Post 8vo, illust. boards, 2s.; cr. 8vo, cloth extra, 3s. 6d.
You Play Me False. Post 8vo, illust. boards, 2s.; cr. 8vo, cloth extra, 3s. 6d.

Collins (Mortimer), Novels by:
Sweet Anne Page. Post 8vo, illustrated boards, 2s.; crown 8vo, cloth extra, 3s. 6d.
Transmigration. Post 8vo, illust. bds., 2s.; crown 8vo, cloth extra, 3s. 6d.
From Midnight to Midnight. Post 8vo, illustrated boards, 2s.; crown 8vo, cloth extra, 3s. 6d.
A Fight with Fortune. Post 8vo, illustrated boards, 2s.

Collins (Wilkie), Novels by.
Each post 8vo, illustrated boards, 2s; cloth limp, 2s. 6d.; or crown 8vo, cloth extra, Illustrated, 3s. 6d.

Antonina. Illust. by A. CONCANEN.

Basil. Illustrated by Sir JOHN GILBERT and J. MAHONEY.

Hide and Seek. Illustrated by Sir JOHN GILBERT and J. MAHONEY.

The Dead Secret. Illustrated by Sir JOHN GILBERT and A. CONCANEN.

Queen of Hearts. Illustrated by Sir JOHN GILBERT and A. CONCANEN.

My Miscellanies. With Illustrations by A. CONCANEN, and a Steel-plate Portrait of WILKIE COLLINS.

The Woman in White. With Illustrations by Sir JOHN GILBERT and F. A. FRASER.

The Moonstone. With Illustrations by G. DU MAURIER and F. A. FRASER.

Man and Wife. Illust. by W. SMALL.

Poor Miss Finch. Illustrated by G. DU MAURIER and EDWARD HUGHES.

Miss or Mrs.? With Illustrations by S. L. FILDES and HENRY WOODS.

The New Magdalen. Illustrated by G. DU MAURIER and C. S. RANDS.

The Frozen Deep. Illustrated by G. DU MAURIER and J. MAHONEY.

The Law and the Lady. Illustrated by S. L. FILDES and SYDNEY HALL.

The Two Destinies.

The Haunted Hotel. Illustrated by ARTHUR HOPKINS.

The Fallen Leaves.

Jezebel's Daughter.

The Black Robe.

Heart and Science: A Story of the Present Time.

"I Say No." Crown 8vo, cloth extra, 3s. 6d. [Shortly.

Colman's Humorous Works:
"Broad Grins," "My Nightgown and Slippers," and other Humorous Works, Prose and Poetical, of GEORGE COLMAN. With Life by G. B. BUCKSTONE, and Frontispiece by HOGARTH. Crown 8vo, cloth extra, gilt, 7s. 6d.

Convalescent Cookery: A Family Handbook. By CATHERINE RYAN. Crown 8vo, 1s.; cloth, 1s. 6d.

Conway (Moncure D.), Works by:
Demonology and Devil-Lore. Two Vols., royal 8vo, with 65 Illusts., 28s.

A Necklace of Stories. Illustrated by W. J. HENNESSY. Square 8vo, cloth extra, 6s.

The Wandering Jew. Crown 8vo, cloth extra, 6s.

Thomas Carlyle: Letters and Recollections. With Illustrations. Crown 8vo, cloth extra, 6s.

Cook (Dutton), Works by:
Hours with the Players. With a Steel Plate Frontispiece. New and Cheaper Edit., cr. 8vo, cloth extra, 6s.

Nights at the Play: A View of the English Stage. New and Cheaper Edition. Crown 8vo, cloth extra, 6s.

Leo: A Novel. Post 8vo, illustrated boards, 2s.

Paul Foster's Daughter. Post 8vo, illustrated boards, 2s.; crown 8vo, cloth extra, 3s. 6d.

Copyright. — A Handbook of English and Foreign Copyright in Literary and Dramatic Works. By SIDNEY JERROLD, of the Middle Temple, Esq., Barrister-at-Law. Post 8vo, cloth limp, 2s. 6d.

Cornwall. — Popular Romances of the West of England; or, The Drolls, Traditions, and Superstitions of Old Cornwall. Collected and Edited by ROBERT HUNT, F.R.S. New and Revised Edition, with Additions, and Two Steel-plate Illustrations by GEORGE CRUIKSHANK. Crown 8vo, cloth extra, 7s. 6d.

Creasy. — Memoirs of Eminent Etonians: with Notices of the Early History of Eton College. By Sir EDWARD CREASY, Author of "The Fifteen Decisive Battles of the World." Crown 8vo, cloth extra, gilt, with 13 Portraits, 7s. 6d.

Cruikshank (George):
The Comic Almanack. Complete in TWO SERIES: The FIRST from 1835 to 1843; the SECOND from 1844 to 1853. A Gathering of the BEST HUMOUR of THACKERAY, HOOD, MAYHEW, ALBERT SMITH, A'BECKETT, ROBERT BROUGH, &c. With 2,000 Woodcuts and Steel Engravings by CRUIKSHANK, HINE, LANDELLS, &c. Crown 8vo, cloth gilt, two very thick volumes, 7s. 6d. each.

CHATTO & WINDUS, PICCADILLY. 7

CRUIKSHANK (G.), continued—
The Life of George Cruikshank. By BLANCHARD JERROLD, Author of "The Life of Napoleon III.," &c. With 84 Illustrations. New and Cheaper Edition, enlarged, with Additional Plates, and a very carefully compiled Bibliography. Crown 8vo, cloth extra, 7s. 6d.

Robinson Crusoe. A beautiful reproduction of Major's Edition, with 37 Woodcuts and Two Steel Plates by GEORGE CRUIKSHANK, choicely printed. Crown 8vo, cloth extra, 7s. 6d. A few Large-Paper copies, printed on hand-made paper, with India proofs of the Illustrations, 36s.

Cussans.—Handbook of Heraldry; with Instructions for Tracing Pedigrees and Deciphering Ancient MSS., &c. By JOHN E. CUSSANS. Entirely New and Revised Edition, illustrated with over 400 Woodcuts and Coloured Plates. Crown 8vo, cloth extra, 7s. 6d.

Cyples.—Hearts of Gold: A Novel. By WILLIAM CYPLES. Crown 8vo, cloth extra, 3s. 6d.; post 8vo, illustrated boards, 2s.

Daniel.—Merrie England in the Olden Time. By GEORGE DANIEL. With Illustrations by ROBT. CRUIKSHANK. Crown 8vo, cloth extra, 3s. 6d.

Daudet.—Port Salvation; or, The Evangelist. By ALPHONSE DAUDET. Translated by C. HARRY MELTZER. With Portrait of the Author. Crown 8vo, cloth extra, 3s. 6d.; post 8vo, illust. boards, 2s.

Davenant.—What shall my Son be? Hints for Parents on the Choice of a Profession or Trade for their Sons. By FRANCIS DAVENANT, M.A. Post 8vo, cloth limp, 2s. 6d.

Davies (Dr. N. E.), Works by:
One Thousand Medical Maxims. Crown 8vo, 1s.; cloth, 1s. 6d.
Nursery Hints: A Mother's Guide. Crown 8vo, 1s.; cloth, 1s. 6d.
Aids to Long Life. Crown 8vo, 2s.; cloth limp, 2s. 6d.

Davies' (Sir John) Complete Poetical Works, including Psalms I. to L. in Verse, and other hitherto Unpublished MSS., for the first time Collected and Edited, with Memorial-Introduction and Notes, by the Rev. A. B. GROSART, D.D. Two Vols., crown 8vo, cloth boards 12s.

De Maistre.—A Journey Round My Room. By XAVIER DE MAISTRE. Translated by HENRY ATTWELL. Post 8vo, cloth limp, 2s. 6d.

De Mille.—A Castle in Spain. A Novel. By JAMES DE MILLE. With a Frontispiece. Crown 8vo, cloth extra, 3s. 6d.; post 8vo, illust. bds., 2s.

Derwent (Leith), Novels by:
Crown 8vo, cloth extra, 3s. 6d.; post 8vo, illustrated boards, 2s.
Our Lady of Tears.
Circe's Lovers.

Dickens (Charles), Novels by:
Post 8vo, illustrated boards, 2s. each.
Sketches by Boz. | Nicholas Nickleby.
Pickwick Papers. | Oliver Twist.

The Speeches of Charles Dickens. (*Mayfair Library.*) Post 8vo, cloth limp, 2s. 6d.

The Speeches of Charles Dickens, 1841-1870. With a New Bibliography, revised and enlarged. Edited and Prefaced by RICHARD HERNE SHEPHERD. Crown 8vo, cloth extra, 6s.

About England with Dickens. By ALFRED RIMMER. With 57 Illustrations by C. A. VANDERHOOF, ALFRED RIMMER, and others. Sq. 8vo, cloth extra, 10s. 6d.

Dictionaries.
A Dictionary of Miracles: Imitative, Realistic, and Dogmatic. By the Rev. E. C. BREWER, LL.D. Crown 8vo, cloth extra, 7s. 6d.; hf.-bound, 9s.
The Reader's Handbook of Allusions, References, Plots, and Stories. By the Rev. E. C. BREWER, LL.D. Fourth Edition, revised throughout, with a New Appendix, containing a Complete English Bibliography. Crown 8vo, 1,400 pages, cloth extra, 7s. 6d.
Authors and their Works, with the Dates. Being the Appendices to "The Reader's Handbook," separately printed. By the Rev E. C. BREWER, LL.D. Crown 8vo, cloth limp, 2s.
Familiar Allusions: A Handbook of Miscellaneous Information; including the Names of Celebrated Statues, Paintings, Palaces, Country Seats, Ruins, Churches, Ships, Streets, Clubs, Natural Curiosities, and the like. By WM. A. WHEELER and CHARLES G. WHEELER. Demy 8vo, cloth extra, 7s. 6d.
Short Sayings of Great Men. With Historical and Explanatory Notes. By SAMUEL A. BENT, M.A. Demy 8vo, cloth extra 7s. 6d.

DICTIONARIES, *continued*—

A Dictionary of the Drama: Being a comprehensive Guide to the Plays, Playwrights, Players, and Playhouses of the United Kingdom and America, from the Earliest to the Present Times. By W. DAVENPORT ADAMS. A thick volume, crown 8vo, half-bound, 12s. 6d. [*In preparation.*

The Slang Dictionary: Etymological, Historical, and Anecdotal. Crown 8vo, cloth extra, **6s. 6d.**

Women of the Day: A Biographical Dictionary. By FRANCES HAYS. Cr. 8vo, cloth **extra, 6s.**

Words, Facts, and **Phrases:** A Dictionary of Curious, Quaint, and Out-of-the-Way Matters. By ELIEZER EDWARDS. New and Cheaper Issue. Cr 8vo, cl. ex., 7s. 6d.; hf.-bd., 9s.

Diderot.—The Paradox of Acting. Translated, with Annotations, from Diderot's "Le Paradoxe sur le Comédien," by WALTER HERRIES POLLOCK. With a Preface by HENRY IRVING. Cr. 8vo, in parchment, 4s. 6d.

Dobson (W. T.), Works by:
Literary Frivolities, Fancies, Follies, and Frolics. Post 8vo, cl. lp., 2s. 6d.
Poetical Ingenuities and Eccentricities. Post 8vo, cloth limp, 2s. 6d.

Doran. — Memories of our Great Towns; with Anecdotic Gleanings concerning their Worthies and their Oddities. By Dr. JOHN DORAN, F.S.A. With 38 Illustrations. New and Cheaper Ed., cr 8vo, cl. ex., 7s. 6d.

Drama, A Dictionary of the. Being a comprehensive Guide to the Plays, Playwrights, Players, and Playhouses of the United Kingdom and America, from the Earliest to the Present Times. By W. DAVENPORT ADAMS. (Uniform with BREWER'S "Reader's **Handbook.**") Crown 8vo, half-bound, **12s. 6d.** [*In preparation.*

Dramatists, The Old. Cr. 8vo, cl. ex., Vignette Portraits, 6s. per Vol.
Ben Jonson's Works. With Notes Critical and Explanatory, and a Biographical Memoir by WM GIFFORD. Edit. by Col. CUNNINGHAM. 3 Vols.
Chapman's Works. Complete in Three Vols. Vol. I. contains the Plays complete, including doubtful ones; Vol. II., Poems and Minor Translations.with IntroductoryEssay by A.C. SWINBURNE; Vol.III., Translations of the Iliad and Odyssey.
Marlowe's Works. Including his Translations. Edited, with Notes and Introduction, by Col. CUNNINGHAM. One Vol.

DRAMATISTS, THE OLD, *continued*—
Massinger's Plays. From the Text of WILLIAM GIFFORD. Edited by Col. CUNNINGHAM. One Vol.

Dyer. — The Folk-Lore of Plants. By T. F. THISELTON DYER, M.A., &c. Crown 8vo, cloth extra, 7s. 6d. [*In preparation.*

Early English Poets. Edited, with Introductions and Annotations, by Rev. A. B. GROSART, D.D. Crown 8vo, cloth boards, 6s. per Volume.
Fletcher's (Giles, B.D.) Complete Poems. One Vol.
Davies' (Sir John) Complete Poetical Works. Two Vols.
Herrick's (Robert) Complete Collected Poems. Three Vols.
Sidney's (Sir Philip) Complete Poetical Works. Three Vols.

Herbert (Lord) of Cherbury's Poems. Edited, with Introduction, by J. CHURTON COLLINS. Crown 8vo, parchment, 8s.

Edwardes (Mrs. A.), Novels by:
A Point of Honour. Post 8vo, illustrated boards, 2s.
Archie Lovell. Post 8vo, illust. bds., 2s.; crown 8vo, cloth extra, 3s. 6d.

Eggleston.—Roxy: A Novel. By EDWARD EGGLESTON. Post 8vo, illust. boards, 2s.; cr. 8vo, cloth extra, 3s. 6d.

Emanuel.—On Diamonds and Precious Stones: their History, Value, and Properties; with Simple Tests for ascertaining their Reality. By HARRY EMANUEL, F.R.G.S. With numerous Illustrations, tinted and plain. Crown 8vo, cloth extra, gilt, 6s.

Englishman's House, The: A Practical Guide to all interested in Selecting or Building a House, with full Estimates of Cost, Quantities, &c. By C. J. RICHARDSON. Third Edition. Nearly 600 Illusts. Cr. 8vo, cl. ex., 7s.6d.

Ewald (Alex. Charles, F.S.A.), Works by:
Stories from the State Papers. With an Autotype Facsimile. Crown 8vo, cloth extra, 6s.
The Life and Times of Prince Charles Stuart, Count of Albany, commonly called the Young Pretender. From the State Papers and other Sources, New and Cheaper Edition, with a Portrait, crown 8vo, cloth extra, 7s. 6d.
Studies Re-studied: Historical Sketches from Original Sources. Demy 8vo, cloth extra, 12s.

Eyes, The.—How to Use our Eyes, and How to Preserve Them. By JOHN BROWNING, F.R.A.S., &c. With 52 Illustrations. 1s.; cloth, 1s. 6d.

Fairholt.—Tobacco: Its History and Associations; with an Account of the Plant and its Manufacture, and its Modes of Use in all Ages and Countries. By F. W. FAIRHOLT, F.S.A. With Coloured Frontispiece and upwards of 100 Illustrations by the Author. Cr. 8vo, cl ex., 6s.

Familiar Allusions: A Handbook of Miscellaneous Information; including the Names of Celebrated Statues, Paintings, Palaces, Country Seats, Ruins, Churches, Ships, Streets, Clubs, Natural Curiosities, and the like. By WILLIAM A. WHEELER, Author of "Noted Names of Fiction;" and CHARLES G. WHEELER. Demy 8vo, cloth extra, 7s. 6d.

Faraday (Michael), Works by:
The Chemical History of a Candle: Lectures delivered before a Juvenile Audience at the Royal Institution. Edited by WILLIAM CROOKES, F.C.S. Post 8vo, cloth extra, with numerous Illustrations, 4s. 6d.
On the Various Forces of Nature, and their Relations to each other: Lectures delivered before a Juvenile Audience at the Royal Institution. Edited by WILLIAM CROOKES, F.C.S. Post 8vo, cloth extra, with numerous Illustrations, 4s. 6d.

Farrer.—Military Manners and Customs. By J. A. FARRER, Author of "Primitive Manners and Customs," &c. Crown 8vo, cloth extra, 6s.

Fin-Bec.—The Cupboard Papers: Observations on the Art of Living and Dining. By FIN-BEC. Post 8vo, cloth limp, 2s. 6d.

Fitzgerald (Percy), Works by:
The Recreations of a Literary Man; or, Does Writing Pay? With Recollections of some Literary Men, and a View of a Literary Man's Working Life. Cr. 8vo, cloth extra, 6s.
The World Behind the Scenes. Crown 8vo, cloth extra, 3s. 6d.
Little Essays: Passages from the Letters of CHARLES LAMB. Post 8vo, cloth limp, 2s. 6d.

Post 8vo, illustrated boards, 2s. each.
Bella Donna. | Never Forgotten.
The Second Mrs. Tillotson.
Polly.
Seventy-five Brooke Street.
The Lady of Brantome.

Fletcher's (Giles, B.D.) Complete Poems: Christ's Victorie in Heaven, Christ's Victorie on Earth, Christ's Triumph over Death, and Minor Poems. With Memorial-Introduction and Notes by the Rev. A. B. GROSART, D.D. Cr. 8vo, cloth bds., 6s.

Fonblanque.—Filthy Lucre: A Novel. By ALBANY DE FONBLANQUE. Post 8vo, illustrated boards, 2s.

Francillon (R. E.), Novels by:
Crown 8vo, cloth extra, 3s. 6d. each; post 8vo, illust. boards, 2s. each.
Olympia. | Queen Cophetua.
One by One. | A Real Queen.
Esther's Glove. Fcap. 8vo, picture cover, 1s.

French Literature, History of. By HENRY VAN LAUN. Complete in 3 Vols., demy 8vo. cl. bds., 7s. 6d. each.

Frere.—Pandurang Hari; or, Memoirs of a Hindoo. With a Preface by Sir H. BARTLE FRERE, G.C.S.I., &c. Crown 8vo, cloth extra, 3s. 6d.; post 8vo, illustrated boards, 2s.

Friswell.—One of Two: A Novel. By HAIN FRISWELL. Post 8vo, illustrated boards, 2s.

Frost (Thomas), Works by:
Crown 8vo, cloth extra, 3s. 6d. each.
Circus Life and Circus Celebrities.
The Lives of the Conjurers.
The Old Showmen and the Old London Fairs.

Fry.—Royal Guide to the London Charities, 1885-6. By HERBERT FRY. Showing their Name, Date of Foundation, Objects, Income, Officials, &c. Published Annually. Crown 8vo, cloth, 1s. 6d. [*Shortly.*

Gardening Books:
A Year's Work in Garden and Greenhouse: Practical Advice to Amateur Gardeners as to the Management of the Flower, Fruit, and Frame Garden. By GEORGE GLENNY. Post 8vo, 1s.: cloth, 1s. 6d.
Our Kitchen Garden: The Plants we Grow, and How we Cook Them. By TOM JERROLD. Post 8vo, 1s.; cloth limp, 1s. 6d.
Household Horticulture: A Gossip about Flowers. By TOM and JANE JERROLD. Illustrated. Post 8vo, 1s.; cloth limp, 1s. 6d.
The Garden that Paid the Rent. By TOM JERROLD. Fcap. 8vo, illustrated cover, 1s.; cloth limp, 1s. 6d.
My Garden Wild, and What I Grew there. By F. G. HEATH. Crown 8vo, cloth extra, 5s.; gilt edges, 6s.

Garrett.—**The Capel Girls: A Novel.** By EDWARD GARRETT. Post 8vo, illust. bds., 2s.; cr. 8vo, cl. ex., 3s. 6d.

Gentleman's Magazine (The) for 1885. One Shilling Monthly. A New Serial Story, entitled "The Unforeseen," by ALICE O'HANLON, begins in the JANUARY Number. "Science Notes," by W. MATTIEU WILLIAMS, F.R.A.S., and "Table Talk," by SYLVANUS URBAN, are also continued monthly.

*** *Now ready, the* **Volume for** JULY to DECEMBER, 1884, *cloth extra, price* 8s. 6d.; *Cases for binding*, 2s. *each*.

German Popular Stories. Collected by the Brothers GRIMM, and Translated by EDGAR TAYLOR. Edited, with an Introduction, by JOHN RUSKIN. With 22 Illustrations on Steel by GEORGE CRUIKSHANK. Square 8vo, cloth extra, 6s. 6d.; gilt edges, 7s. 6d.

Gibbon (Charles), Novels by:
Crown 8vo, cloth extra, 3s. 6d. each; post 8vo, illustrated boards, 2s. each.

Robin Gray.	In Pastures Green
For Lack of Gold.	Braes of Yarrow.
What will the World Say?	The Flower of the Forest.
In Honour Bound.	A Heart's Problem.
In Love and War.	
For the King.	The Golden Shaft.
Queen of the Meadow.	Of High Degree.

Post 8vo, illustrated boards, 2s.
The Dead Heart.

Crown 8vo, cloth extra, 3s. 6d. each.
Fancy Free. | Loving a Dream.

By Mead and Stream. Three Vols., crown 8vo, 31s. 6d.
A Hard Knot. Three Vols., crown 8vo, 31s. 6d.
Heart's Delight. Three Vols., crown 8vo, 31s. 6d. [*In the press.*

Gilbert (William), Novels by:
Post 8vo, illustrated boards, 2s. each.
Dr. Austin's Guests.
The Wizard of the Mountain.
James Duke, Costermonger.

Gilbert (W. S.), Original Plays by: In Two Series, each complete in itself, price 2s. 6d. each.
The FIRST SERIES contains—The Wicked World—Pygmalion and Galatea—Charity—The Princess—The Palace of Truth—Trial by Jury.
The SECOND SERIES contains—Broken Hearts—Engaged—Sweethearts—Gretchen—Dan'l Druce—Tom Cobb—H.M.S. Pinafore—The Sorcerer—The Pirates of Penzance.

Glenny.—**A Year's Work in Garden and Greenhouse:** Practical Advice to Amateur Gardeners as to the Management of the Flower, Fruit, and Frame Garden. By GEORGE GLENNY. Post 8vo, 1s.; cloth, 1s. 6d.

Godwin.—**Lives of the Necromancers.** By WILLIAM GODWIN. Post 8vo, cloth limp, 2s.

Golden Library, The:
Square 16mo (Tauchnitz size), cloth limp, 2s. per volume.

Bayard Taylor's Diversions of the Echo Club.

Bennett's (Dr. W. C.) Ballad History of England.

Bennett's (Dr.) Songs for Sailors.

Byron's Don Juan.

Godwin's (William) Lives of the Necromancers.

Holmes's Autocrat of the Breakfast Table. With an Introduction by G. A. SALA.

Holmes's Professor at the Breakfast Table.

Hood's Whims and Oddities. Complete. All the original Illustrations.

Irving's (Washington) Tales of a Traveller.

Irving's (Washington) Tales of the Alhambra.

Jesse's (Edward) Scenes and Occupations of a Country Life.

Lamb's Essays of Elia. Both Series Complete in One Vol.

Leigh Hunt's Essays: A Tale for a Chimney Corner, and other Pieces. With Portrait, and Introduction by EDMUND OLLIER.

Mallory's (Sir Thomas) Mort d'Arthur: The Stories of King Arthur and of the Knights of the Round Table. Edited by B. MONTGOMERIE RANKING.

Pascal's Provincial Letters. A New Translation, with Historical Introduction and Notes, by T. M'CRIE, D.D.

Pope's Poetical Works. Complete.

Rochefoucauld's Maxims and Moral Reflections. With Notes, and Introductory Essay by SAINTE-BEUVE.

St. Pierre's Paul and Virginia, and The Indian Cottage. Edited, with Life, by the Rev. E. CLARKE.

Shelley's Early Poems, and Queen Mab. With Essay by LEIGH HUNT.

Shelley's Later Poems: Laon and Cythna, &c.

Shelley's Posthumous Poems, the Shelley Papers, &c.

GOLDEN LIBRARY, THE, continued—
Shelley's Prose Works, including A Refutation of Deism, Zastrozzi, St. Irvyne, &c.
White's Natural History of Selborne. Edited, with Additions, by THOMAS BROWN, F.L.S.

Golden Treasury of Thought, The: An ENCYCLOPÆDIA OF QUOTATIONS from Writers of all Times and Countries. Selected and Edited by THEODORE TAYLOR. Crown 8vo, cloth gilt and gilt edges, 7s. 6d.

Gordon Cumming (C. F.), Works by:
In the Hebrides. With Autotype Facsimile and numerous full-page Illustrations. Demy 8vo, cloth extra, 8s. 6d.
In the Himalayas and on the Indian Plains. With numerous Illustrations. Demy 8vo, cloth extra, 8s. 6d.
Via Cornwall to Egypt. With a Photogravure Frontispiece. Demy 8vo, cloth extra, 7s. 6d.

Graham. — The Professor's Wife: A Story. By LEONARD GRAHAM. Fcap. 8vo, picture cover, 1s.; cloth extra, 2s. 6d.

Greeks and Romans, The Life of the, Described from Antique Monuments. By ERNST GUHL and W. KONER. Translated from the Third German Edition, and Edited by Dr. F. HUEFFER. With 545 Illustrations. New and Cheaper Edition, demy 8vo, cloth extra, 7s. 6d.

Greenwood (James), Works by:
The Wilds of London. Crown 8vo, cloth extra, 3s. 6d.
Low-Life Deeps: An Account of the Strange Fish to be Found There. Crown 8vo, cloth extra, 3s. 6d.
Dick Temple A Novel. Post 8vo, illustrated boards, 2s.

Guyot. — The Earth and Man; or, Physical Geography in its relation to the History of Mankind. By ARNOLD GUYOT. With Additions by Professors AGASSIZ, PIERCE, and GRAY; 12 Maps and Engravings on Steel, some Coloured, and copious Index. Crown 8vo, cloth extra, gilt, 4s. 6d.

Hair (The): Its Treatment in Health, Weakness, and Disease. Translated from the German of Dr. J. PINCUS. Crown 8vo, 1s.; cloth, 1s. 6d.

Hake (Dr. Thomas Gordon), Poems by:
Maiden Ecstasy. Small 4to, cloth extra, 8s.

HAKE'S (Dr. T. G.) POEMS, continued—
New Symbols. Cr. 8vo, cloth extra, 6s.
Legends of the Morrow. Crown 8vo, cloth extra, 6s.
The Serpent Play. Crown 8vo, cloth extra, 6s.

Hall. — Sketches of Irish Character. By Mrs. S. C. HALL. With numerous Illustrations on Steel and Wood by MACLISE, GILBERT, HARVEY, and G. CRUIKSHANK. Medium 8vo, cloth extra, gilt, 7s. 6d.

Hall Caine. — The Shadow of a Crime: A Novel. By HALL CAINE. Cr. 8vo, cloth extra, 3s. 6d. [Shortly.

Halliday. — Every-day Papers. By ANDREW HALLIDAY. Post 8vo, illustrated boards, 2s.

Handwriting, The Philosophy of. With over 100 Facsimiles and Explanatory Text. By DON FELIX DE SALAMANCA. Post 8vo, cl. limp, 2s. 6d.

Hanky-Panky: A Collection of Very Easy Tricks, Very Difficult Tricks, White Magic, Sleight of Hand, &c. Edited by W. H. CREMER. With 200 Illusts. Crown 8vo, cloth extra, 4s. 6d.

Hardy (Lady Duffus). — Paul Wynter's Sacrifice: A Story. By Lady DUFFUS HARDY. Post 8vo, illust. boards, 2s.

Hardy (Thomas). — Under the Greenwood Tree. By THOMAS HARDY, Author of "Far from the Madding Crowd." Crown 8vo, cloth extra, 3s. 6d.; post 8vo, illustrated bds., 2s.

Haweis (Mrs. H. R.), Works by:
The Art of Dress. With numerous Illustrations. Small 8vo, illustrated cover, 1s.; cloth limp, 1s. 6d.
The Art of Beauty. New and Cheaper Edition. Crown 8vo, cloth extra, with Coloured Frontispiece and Illustrations, 6s.
The Art of Decoration. Square 8vo, handsomely bound and profusely Illustrated, 10s. 6d.
Chaucer for Children: A Golden Key. With Eight Coloured Pictures and numerous Woodcuts. New Edition, small 4to, cloth extra, 6s.
Chaucer for Schools. Demy 8vo, cloth limp, 2s. 6d.

Haweis (Rev. H. R.). — American Humorists. Including WASHINGTON IRVING, OLIVER WENDELL HOLMES, JAMES RUSSELL LOWELL, ARTEMUS WARD, MARK TWAIN, and BRET HARTE. By the Rev. H. R. HAWEIS, M.A. Crown 8vo, cloth extra, 6s.

Hawthorne (Julian), Novels by.
Crown 8vo, cloth extra, 3s. 6d. each;
post 8vo, illustrated boards, 2s. each.

| Garth. | Sebastian Strome. |
| Ellice Quentin. | Dust. |

Prince Saroni's Wife.
Fortune's Fool.
Beatrix Randolph.

> Mrs. Gainsborough's Diamonds.
> Fcap. 8vo, illustrated cover, 1s.;
> cloth extra, 2s. 6d.

> Miss Cadogna. Crown 8vo, cloth extra,
> 3s. 6d. each.

IMPORTANT NEW BIOGRAPHY.

Hawthorne (Nathaniel) and his Wife. By JULIAN HAWTHORNE. With 6 Steel-plate Portraits. Two Vols., crown 8vo, cloth extra, 24s.

> [Twenty-five copies of an *Edition de Luxe*, printed on the best hand-made paper, large 8vo size, and with India proofs of the Illustrations, are reserved for sale in England, price 48s. per set. Immediate application should be made by anyone desiring a copy of this special and very limited Edition.]

Hays.—Women of the Day: A Biographical Dictionary of Notable Contemporaries. By FRANCES HAYS. Crown 8vo, cloth extra, 5s.

Heath (F. G.).—My Garden Wild, and What I Grew There. By FRANCIS GEORGE HEATH, Author of "The Fern World," &c. Crown 8vo, cl. ex., 5s.; cl. gilt, gilt edges, 6s.

Helps (Sir Arthur), Works by:
Animals and their Masters. Post 8vo, cloth limp, 2s. 6d.
Social Pressure. Post 8vo, cloth limp, 2s. 6d.
Ivan de Biron: A Novel. Crown 8vo, cloth extra, 3s. 6d.; post 8vo, illustrated boards, 2s.

Heptalogia (The); or, The Seven against Sense. A Cap with Seven Bells. Cr. 8vo, cloth extra, 6s.

Herbert.—The Poems of Lord Herbert of Cherbury. Edited, with Introduction, by J. CHURTON COLLINS. Crown 8vo, bound in parchment, 8s.

Herrick's (Robert) Hesperides, Noble Numbers, and Complete Collected Poems. With Memorial-Introduction and Notes by the Rev. A. B. GROSART, D.D., Steel Portrait, Index of First Lines, and Glossarial Index, &c. Three Vols., crown 8vo, cloth, 18s.

Hesse-Wartegg (Chevalier Ernst von), Works by:
Tunis: The Land and the People. With 22 Illustrations. Crown 8vo, cloth extra, 3s. 6d.
The New South-West: Travelling Sketches from Kansas, New Mexico, Arizona, and Northern Mexico. With 100 fine Illustrations and Three Maps. Demy 8vo, cloth extra, 14s. [*In preparation.*

Hindley (Charles), Works by:
Crown 8vo, cloth extra, 3s. 6d. each.
Tavern Anecdotes and Sayings: Including the Origin of Signs, and Reminiscences connected with Taverns, Coffee Houses, Clubs, &c. With Illustrations.
The Life and Adventures of a Cheap Jack. By One of the Fraternity. Edited by CHARLES HINDLEY.

Hoey.—The Lover's Creed. By Mrs. CASHEL HOEY. With 12 Illustrations by P. MACNAB. Three Vols., crown 8vo, 31s. 6d.

Holmes (O. Wendell), Works by:
The Autocrat of the Breakfast-Table. Illustrated by J. GORDON THOMSON. Post 8vo, cloth limp, 2s. 6d.; another Edition in smaller type, with an Introduction by G. A. SALA. Post 8vo, cloth limp, 2s.
The Professor at the Breakfast-Table; with the Story of Iris. Post 8vo, cloth limp, 2s.

Holmes.—The Science of Voice Production and Voice Preservation: A Popular Manual for the Use of Speakers and Singers. By GORDON HOLMES, M.D. With Illustrations. Crown 8vo, 1s.; cloth, 1s. 6d.

Hood (Thomas):
Hood's Choice Works, in Prose and Verse. Including the Cream of the Comic Annuals. With Life of the Author, Portrait, and 200 Illustrations. Crown 8vo, cloth extra, 7s. 6d.
Hood's Whims and Oddities. Complete. With all the original Illustrations. Post 8vo, cloth limp, 2s.

Hood (Tom), Works by:
From Nowhere to the North Pole: A Noah's Arkæological Narrative. With 25 Illustrations by W. BRUNTON and E. C. BARNES. Square crown 8vo, cloth extra, gilt edges, 6s.
A Golden Heart: A Novel. Post 8vo, illustrated boards, 2s.

Hook's (Theodore) Choice Humorous Works, including his Ludicrous Adventures, Bons Mots, Puns and Hoaxes. With a New Life of the Author, Portraits, Facsimiles, and Illusts. Cr. 8vo, cl. extra, gilt, 7s. 6d.

Hooper.—The House of Raby: A Novel. By Mrs. GEORGE HOOPER. Post 8vo, illustrated boards, 2s.

Horne.—Orion: An Epic Poem, in Three Books. By RICHARD HENGIST HORNE. With Photographic Portrait from a Medallion by SUMMERS. Tenth Edition, crown 8vo, cloth extra, 7s.

Howell.—Conflicts of Capital and Labour, Historically and Economically considered : Being a History and Review of the Trade Unions of Great Britain, showing their Origin, Progress, Constitution, and Objects, in their Political, Social, Economical, and Industrial Aspects. By GEORGE HOWELL. Cr. 8vo, cloth extra, 7s. 6d.

Hugo. — The Hunchback of Notre Dame. By VICTOR HUGO. Post 8vo, illustrated boards, 2s.

Hunt.—Essays by Leigh Hunt. A Tale for a Chimney Corner, and other Pieces. With Portrait and Introduction by EDMUND OLLIER. Post 8vo, cloth limp, 2s.

Hunt (Mrs. Alfred), Novels by: Crown 8vo, cloth extra, 3s. 6d. each; post 8vo, illustrated boards, 2s. each.
Thornicroft's Model.
The Leaden Casket.
Self-Condemned.

Ingelow.—Fated to be Free: A Novel. By JEAN INGELOW. Crown 8vo, cloth extra, 3s. 6d.; post 8vo, illustrated boards, 2s.

Irish Wit and Humour, Songs of. Collected and Edited by A. PERCEVAL GRAVES. Post 8vo, cl. limp, 2s. 6d.

Irving (Washington),Works by:
Post 8vo, cloth limp, 2s. each.
Tales of a Traveller.
Tales of the Alhambra.

Janvier.—Practical Keramics for Students. By CATHERINE A. JANVIER. Crown 8vo, cloth extra, 6s.

Jay (Harriett), Novels by. Each crown 8vo, cloth extra, 3s. 6d.; or post 8vo, illustrated boards, 2s.
The Dark Colleen.
The Queen of Connaught.

Jefferies (Richard), Works by:
Nature near London. Crown 8vo, cloth extra, 6s.
The Life of the Fields. Crown 8vo, cloth extra, 6s.

Jennings (H. J.), Works by:
Curiosities of Criticism. Post 8vo, cloth limp, 2s. 6d.
Lord Tennyson: A Biographical Sketch. With a Photograph-Portrait. Crown 8vo, cloth extra, 6s.

Jennings (Hargrave). — The Rosicrucians: Their Rites and Mysteries. With Chapters on the Ancient Fire and Serpent Worshippers. By HARGRAVE JENNINGS. With Five full-page Plates and upwards of 300 Illustrations. A New Edition, crown 8vo, cloth extra, 7s. 6d.

Jerrold (Tom), Works by:
The Garden that Paid the Rent. By TOM JERROLD. Fcap. 8vo, illustrated cover, 1s.; cloth limp, 1s. 6d.
Household Horticulture: A Gossip about Flowers. By TOM and JANE JERROLD. Illustrated. Post 8vo, 1s.; cloth, limp, 1s. 6d.
Our Kitchen Garden: The Plants we Grow, and How we Cook Them. By TOM JERROLD. Post 8vo, 1s.; cloth limp, 1s. 6d.

Jesse.—Scenes and Occupations of a Country Life. By EDWARD JESSE. Post 8vo, cloth limp, 2s.

Jones (Wm., F.S.A.), Works by:
Finger-Ring Lore: Historical, Legendary, and Anecdotal. With over 200 Illusts. Cr. 8vo, cl. extra, 7s. 6d.
Credulities, Past and Present; including the Sea and Seamen, Miners, Talismans, Word and Letter Divination, Exorcising and Blessing of Animals, Birds, Eggs, Luck, &c. With an Etched Frontispiece. Crown 8vo, cloth extra, 7s. 6d.
Crowns and Coronations: A History of Regalia in all Times and Countries. With One Hundred Illustrations. Cr. 8vo, cloth extra, 7s. 6d.

Jonson's (Ben) Works. With Notes Critical and Explanatory, and a Biographical Memoir by WILLIAM GIFFORD. Edited by Colonel CUNNINGHAM. Three Vols., crown 8vo, cloth extra, 18s.; or separately, 6s. each.

Josephus,The CompleteWorks of. Translated by WHISTON. Containing both "The Antiquities of the Jews" and "The Wars of the Jews." Two Vols., 8vo, with 52 Illustrations and Maps, cloth extra, gilt, 14s.

Kavanagh.—**The Pearl Fountain**, and other Fairy Stories. By BRIDGET and JULIA KAVANAGH. With Thirty Illustrations by J. MOYR SMITH. Small 8vo, cloth gilt, 6s.

Kempt.—**Pencil and Palette:** Chapters on Art and Artists. By ROBERT KEMPT. Post 8vo, cloth limp, 2s. 6d.

Kingsley (Henry), Novels by: Each crown 8vo, cloth extra, 3s. 6d.; or post 8vo, illustrated boards, 2s.

Oakshott Castle. | Number Seventeen

Knight.—**The Patient's Vade Mecum: How to get** most Benefit from Medical **Advice.** By WILLIAM KNIGHT, **M.R.C.S.**, and EDWARD KNIGHT, L.R.C.P. Crown **8vo, 1s.;** cloth, **1s. 6d.**

Lamb (Charles):

Mary and Charles Lamb: Their Poems, Letters, and Remains. With Reminiscences and Notes by W. CAREW HAZLITT. With HANCOCK's Portrait of the Essayist, Facsimiles of the Title-pages of the rare First Editions of Lamb's and Coleridge's Works, and numerous Illustrations. Crown 8vo, cloth extra, 10s. 6d.

Lamb's Complete Works, in Prose and Verse, reprinted from the Original Editions, with many Pieces hitherto unpublished. Edited, with Notes and Introduction, by R. H. SHEPHERD. With Two Portraits and Facsimile **of** Page of the " Essay on Roast Pig." Cr. 8vo, cloth extra, 7s. 6d.

The Essays of Elia. Complete Edition. Post 8vo, cloth extra, 2s.

Poetry for Children, and Prince Dorus. By CHARLES LAMB. Carefully reprinted **from** unique copies. Small 8vo, cloth **extra, 5s.**

Little **Essays:** Sketches and Characters. By **CHARLES** LAMB. Selected from **his Letters** by PERCY FITZ-GERALD. Post **8vo,** cloth limp, 2s. 6d.

Lane's Arabian Nights, &c.:

The Thousand and One Nights: commonly called, in England, " THE ARABIAN NIGHTS' ENTERTAINMENTS." A New Translation from the Arabic, with copious Notes, by EDWARD WILLIAM LANE. Illustrated by many hundred Engravings on Wood, from Original Designs by WM. HARVEY. A New Edition, from a Copy annotated by the Translator, edited by his Nephew, EDWARD STANLEY POOLE. With a Preface by STANLEY LANE-POOLE. Three Vols., demy 8vo, cloth extra, 7s. 6d. each.

LANE'S ARABIAN NIGHTS, *continued—*

Arabian Society in the Middle Ages: Studies from "The Thousand and One Nights." By EDWARD WILLIAM LANE, Author of "The Modern Egyptians," &c. Edited by STANLEY LANE-POOLE. Cr. 8vo, cloth extra, 6s.

Lares and Penates; or, The Background of Life. By FLORENCE CADDY. Crown 8vo, cloth extra, 6s.

Larwood (Jacob), Works by:

The Story of the London Parks. With Illustrations. Crown 8vo, cloth extra, 3s. 6d.

Clerical Anecdotes. Post 8vo, **cloth** limp, 2s. 6d.

Forensic Anecdotes. Post 8vo, cloth limp, 2s. 6d.

Theatrical Anecdotes. Post 8vo, cloth limp, 2s. 6d.

Leigh (Henry S.), Works by:

Carols of Cockayne. With numerous Illustrations. Post 8vo, cloth limp, 2s. 6d.

Jeux d'Esprit. Collected and Edited by HENRY S. LEIGH. Post 8vo, cloth limp, 2s. 6d.

Life in London; or, The History of Jerry Hawthorn and Corinthian Tom. With the whole of CRUIKSHANK's Illustrations, in Colours, after the Originals. Crown 8vo, cloth extra, 7s. 6d.

Linton (E. Lynn), Works by:

Post 8vo, cloth limp, 2s. 6d. each.

Witch Stories.

The True Story of Joshua Davidson.

Ourselves: Essays on Women.

Crown 8vo, cloth extra, 3s. 6d. each; post 8vo, illustrated boards, 2s. each.

Patricia Kemball.

The Atonement of Leam Dundas.

The World Well Lost.

Under which Lord?

With a Silken Thread.

The Rebel of the Family.

"My Love!"

Ione.

Locks and Keys.—On the Development and Distribution of Primitive Locks and Keys. By Lieut.-Gen. PITT-RIVERS, F.R.S. With numerous Illustrations. Demy 4to, half Roxburghe, 16s.

Longfellow:

Longfellow's Complete Prose Works. Including "Outre Mer," "Hyperion," "Kavanagh," "The Poets and Poetry of Europe," and "Driftwood." With Portrait and Illustrations by VALENTINE BROMLEY. Crown 8vo, cloth extra, 7s. 6d.

Longfellow's Poetical Works. Carefully Reprinted from the Original Editions. With numerous fine Illustrations on Steel and Wood. Crown 8vo, cloth extra, 7s. 6d.

Long Life, Aids to: A Medical, Dietetic, and General Guide in Health and Disease. By N. E. DAVIES, L.R.C.P. Crown 8vo, 2s; cloth limp, 2s. 6d.

Lucy.—Gideon Fleyce: A Novel. By HENRY W. LUCY. Crown 8vo, cl. extra, 3s. 6d.; post 8vo, illust. bds., 2s.

Lusiad (The) of Camoens. Translated into English Spenserian Verse by ROBERT FFRENCH DUFF. Demy 8vo, with Fourteen full-page Plates, cloth boards, 18s.

McCarthy (Justin, M.P.), Works by:

A History of Our Own Times, from the Accession of Queen Victoria to the General Election of 1880. Four Vols. demy 8vo, cloth extra, 12s. each.—Also a POPULAR EDITION, in Four Vols. cr. 8vo, cl. extra, 6s. each.

A Short History of Our Own Times. One Vol., crown 8vo, cloth extra, 6s.

History of the Four Georges. Four Vols. demy 8vo, cloth extra, 12s. each.   [Vol. I. now ready.

Crown 8vo, cloth extra, 3s. 6d. each; post 8vo, illustrated boards, 2s. each.
Dear Lady Disdain.
The Waterdale Neighbours.
My Enemy's Daughter.
A Fair Saxon.
Linley Rochford.
Miss Misanthrope.
Donna Quixote.
The Comet of a Season.
Maid of Athens.

McCarthy (Justin H., M.P.), Works by:

An Outline of the History of Ireland, from the Earliest Times to the Present Day. Cr. 8vo, 1s.; cloth, 1s. 6d.

England under Gladstone. Crown 8vo, cloth extra, 6s.

MacDonald (George, LL.D.), Works by:

The Princess and Curdie. With 11 Illustrations by JAMES ALLEN. Small crown 8vo, cloth extra, 5s.

Gutta-Percha Willie, the Working Genius. With 9 Illustrations by ARTHUR HUGHES. Square 8vo, cloth extra, 3s. 6d.

Paul Faber, Surgeon. With a Frontispiece by J. E. MILLAIS. Crown 8vo, cloth extra, 3s. 6d.; post 8vo, illustrated boards, 2s.

Thomas Wingfold, Curate. With a Frontispiece by C. J. STANILAND. Crown 8vo, cloth extra, 3s. 6d.; post 8vo, illustrated boards, 2s.

Macdonell.—Quaker Cousins: A Novel. By AGNES MACDONELL. Crown 8vo, cloth extra, 3s. 6d.; post 8vo, illustrated boards, 2s.

Macgregor. — Pastimes and Players. Notes on Popular Games. By ROBERT MACGREGOR. Post 8vo, cloth limp, 2s. 6d.

Maclise Portrait-Gallery (The) of Illustrious Literary Characters; with Memoirs—Biographical, Critical, Bibliographical, and Anecdotal—illustrative of the Literature of the former half of the Present Century. By WILLIAM BATES, B.A. With 85 Portraits printed on an India Tint. Crown 8vo, cloth extra, 7s. 6d.

Macquoid (Mrs.), Works by:

In the Ardennes. With 50 fine Illustrations by THOMAS R. MACQUOID. Square 8vo, cloth extra, 10s. 6d.

Pictures and Legends from Normandy and Brittany. With numerous Illustrations by THOMAS R. MACQUOID. Square 8vo, cloth gilt, 10s. 6d.

Through Normandy. With 90 Illustrations by T. R. MACQUOID. Square 8vo, cloth extra, 7s. 6d.

Through Brittany. With numerous Illustrations by T. R. MACQUOID. Square 8vo, cloth extra, 7s. 6d.

About Yorkshire. With 67 Illustrations by T. R. MACQUOID, Engraved by SWAIN. Square 8vo, cloth extra, 10s. 6d.

The Evil Eye, and other Stories. Crown 8vo, cloth extra, 3s. 6d.; post 8vo, illustrated boards, 2s.

Lost Rose, and other Stories. Crown 8vo, cloth extra, 3s. 6d.; post 8vo, illustrated boards, 2s.

Mackay.—Interludes and Undertones: or, Music at Twilight. By CHARLES MACKAY, LL.D. Crown 8vo, cloth extra, 6s.

Magic Lantern (The), and its Management: including Full Practical Directions for producing the Limelight, making Oxygen Gas, and preparing Lantern Slides. By T. C. HEPWORTH. With 10 Illustrations. Crown 8vo, 1s ; cloth, 1s. 6d.

Magician's Own Book (The): Performances with Cups and Balls, Eggs, Hats, Handkerchiefs, &c. All from actual Experience. Edited by W. H. CREMER. With 200 Illustrations. Crown 8vo, cloth extra, 4s. 6d.

Magic No Mystery: Tricks with Cards, Dice, Balls, &c., with fully descriptive Directions; the Art of Secret Writing; Training of Performing Animals, &c. With Coloured Frontispiece and many Illustrations. Crown 8vo, cloth extra, 4s. 6d.

Magna Charta. An exact Facsimile of the Original in the British Museum, printed on fine plate paper, 3 feet by 2 feet, with Arms and Seals emblazoned in Gold and Colours. Price 5s.

Mallock (W. H.), Works by:
The New Republic; or, Culture, Faith and Philosophy in an English Country House. Post 8vo, cloth limp, 2s. 6d.; Cheap Edition, illustrated boards, 2s.
The New Paul and Virginia; or, Positivism on an Island. Post 8vo, cloth limp, 2s. 6d.
Poems. Small 4to, bound in parchment, 8s.
Is Life worth Living? Crown 8vo, cloth extra, 6s.

Mallory's (Sir Thomas) Mort d'Arthur: The Stories of King Arthur and of the Knights of the Round Table. Edited by B. MONTGOMERIE RANKING. Post 8vo, cloth limp, 2s.

Marlowe's Works. Including his Translations. Edited, with Notes and Introduction, by Col. CUNNINGHAM. Crown 8vo, cloth extra, 6s.

Marryat (Florence), Novels by:
Crown 8vo, cloth extra, 3s. 6d. each; or, post 8vo, illustrated boards, 2s.
Open! Sesame!
Written in Fire.

Post 8vo, illustrated boards, 2s. each.
A Harvest of Wild Oats.
A Little Stepson.
Fighting the Air.

Masterman.—Half a Dozen Daughters: A Novel. By J. MASTERMAN. Post 8vo, illustrated boards, 2s.

Mark Twain, Works by:
The Choice Works of Mark Twain. Revised and Corrected throughout by the Author. With Life, Portrait, and numerous Illustrations. Crown 8vo, cloth extra, 7s. 6d.
The Adventures of Tom Sawyer. With 111 Illustrations. Crown 8vo, cloth extra, 7s. 6d.
₊ Also a Cheap Edition, post 8vo, illustrated boards, 2s.
An Idle Excursion, and other Sketches. Post 8vo, illustrated boards, 2s.
The Prince and the Pauper. With nearly 200 Illustrations. Crown 8vo, cloth extra, 7s. 6d.
The Innocents Abroad; or, The New Pilgrim's Progress: Being some Account of the Steamship "Quaker City's" Pleasure Excursion to Europe and the Holy Land. With 234 Illustrations. Crown 8vo, cloth extra, 7s. 6d. CHEAP EDITION (under the title of "MARK TWAIN'S PLEASURE TRIP"), post 8vo, illust. boards, 2s.
Roughing It, and The Innocents at Home. With 200 Illustrations by F. A. FRASER. Crown 8vo, cloth extra, 7s. 6d.
The Gilded Age. By MARK TWAIN and CHARLES DUDLEY WARNER. With 212 Illustrations by T. COPPIN. Crown 8vo, cloth extra, 7s. 6d.
A Tramp Abroad. With 314 Illustrations. Crown 8vo, cloth extra, 7s. 6d.; Post 8vo, illustrated boards, 2s.
The Stolen White Elephant, &c. Crown 8vo, cloth extra, 6s.; post 8vo, illustrated boards, 2s.
Life on the Mississippi. With about 300 Original Illustrations. Crown 8vo, cloth extra, 7s. 6d.
The Adventures of Huckleberry Finn. With 174 Illustrations by E. W. KEMBLE. Crown 8vo, cloth extra, 7s. 6d.

Massinger's Plays. From the Text of WILLIAM GIFFORD. Edited by Col. CUNNINGHAM. Crown 8vo, cloth extra, 6s.

Mayhew.—London Characters and the Humorous Side of London Life. By HENRY MAYHEW. With numerous Illustrations. Crown 8vo, cloth extra, 3s. 6d.

Mayfair Library, The:
Post 8vo, cloth limp, 2s. 6d. per Volume.
A Journey Round My Room. By XAVIER DE MAISTRE. Translated by HENRY ATTWELL.
Latter-Day Lyrics. Edited by W. DAVENPORT ADAMS.

MAYFAIR LIBRARY, continued—
  Quips and Quiddities. Selected by W. DAVENPORT ADAMS.
  The Agony Column of "The Times," from 1800 to 1870. Edited, with an Introduction, by ALICE CLAY.
  Balzac's "Comedie Humaine" and its Author. With Translations by H. H. WALKER.
  Melancholy Anatomised: A Popular Abridgment of "Burton's Anatomy of Melancholy."
  Gastronomy as a Fine Art. By BRILLAT-SAVARIN.
  The Speeches of Charles Dickens.
  Literary Frivolities, Fancies, Follies, and Frolics. By W. T. DOBSON.
  Poetical Ingenuities and Eccentricities. Selected and Edited by W. T. DOBSON.
  The Cupboard Papers. By FIN-BEC.
  Original Plays by W. S. GILBERT. FIRST SERIES. Containing: The Wicked World — Pygmalion and Galatea — Charity — The Princess — The Palace of Truth — Trial by Jury.
  Original Plays by W. S. GILBERT. SECOND SERIES. Containing: Broken Hearts — Engaged — Sweethearts — Gretchen — Dan'l Druce — Tom Cobb — H.M.S. Pinafore — The Sorcerer — The Pirates of Penzance.
  Songs of Irish Wit and Humour. Collected and Edited by A. PERCEVAL GRAVES.
  Animals and their Masters. By Sir ARTHUR HELPS.
  Social Pressure. By Sir A. HELPS.
  Curiosities of Criticism. By HENRY J. JENNINGS.
  The Autocrat of the Breakfast-Table. By OLIVER WENDELL HOLMES. Illustrated by J. GORDON THOMSON.
  Pencil and Palette. By ROBERT KEMPT.
  Little Essays: Sketches and Characters. By CHAS. LAMB. Selected from his Letters by PERCY FITZGERALD.
  Clerical Anecdotes. By JACOB LARWOOD.
  Forensic Anecdotes; or, Humour and Curiosities of the Law and Men of Law. By JACOB LARWOOD.
  Theatrical Anecdotes. By JACOB LARWOOD.
  Carols of Cockayne. By HENRY S. LEIGH.
  Jeux d'Esprit. Edited by HENRY S. LEIGH.
  True History of Joshua Davidson. By E. LYNN LINTON.
  Witch Stories. By E. LYNN LINTON.
  Ourselves: Essays on Women. By E. LYNN LINTON.
  Pastimes and Players. By ROBERT MACGREGOR.

MAYFAIR LIBRARY, continued—
  The New Paul and Virginia. By W. H. MALLOCK. [LOCK.
  The New Republic. By W. H. MALPuck on Pegasus. By H. CHOLMONDELEY-PENNELL.
  Pegasus Re-Saddled. By H. CHOLMONDELEY-PENNELL. Illustrated by GEORGE DU MAURIER.
  Muses of Mayfair. Edited by H CHOLMONDELEY-PENNELL.
  Thoreau: His Life and Aims. By H. A. PAGE.
  Puniana. By the Hon. HUGH ROWLEY.
  More Puniana. By the Hon. HUGH ROWLEY.
  The Philosophy of Handwriting. By DON FELIX DE SALAMANCA.
  By Stream and Sea. By WILLIAM SENIOR. [THORNBURY.
  Old Stories Re-told. By WALTER
  Leaves from a Naturalist's Note-Book. By Dr. ANDREW WILSON.

Medicine, Family.—One Thousand Medical Maxims and Surgical Hints, for Infancy, Adult Life, Middle Age, and Old Age. By N. E. DAVIES, L.R.C.P. Lond. Cr. 8vo, 1s.; cl., 1s. 6d.

Merry Circle (The): A Book of New Intellectual Games and Amusements. By CLARA BELLEW. With numerous Illustrations. Crown 8vo, cloth extra, 4s. 6d.

Mexican Mustang (On a). Through Texas, from the Gulf to the Rio Grande. A New Book of American Humour. By ALEX. E. SWEET and J. ARMOY KNOX, Editors of "Texas Siftings." 265 Illusts. Cr 8vo, cloth extra, 7s. 6d.

Middlemass (Jean), Novels by:
  Touch and Go. Crown 8vo, cloth extra, 3s. 6d.; post 8vo, illust. bds., 2s.
  Mr. Dorillion. Post 8vo, illust. bds., 2s.

Miller.—Physiology for the Young; or, The House of Life: Human Physiology, with its application to the Preservation of Health. For use in Classes and Popular Reading. With numerous Illustrations. By Mrs. F. FENWICK MILLER. Small 8vo, cloth limp, 2s. 6d.

Milton (J. L.), Works by:
  The Hygiene of the Skin. A Concise Set of Rules for the Management of the Skin; with Directions for Diet, Wines, Soaps, Baths, &c. Small 8vo, 1s.; cloth extra, 1s. 6d.
  The Bath in Diseases of the Skin. Small 8vo, 1s.; cloth extra, 1s. 6d.
  The Laws of Life, and their Relation to Diseases of the Skin. Small 8vo, 1s.; cloth extra, 1s. 6d.

Moncrieff.—The Abdication; or, Time Tries All. An Historical Drama. By W. D. SCOTT-MONCRIEFF. With Seven Etchings by JOHN PETTIE, R.A., W. Q. ORCHARDSON, R.A., J. MACWHIRTER, A.R.A., COLIN HUNTER, R. MACBETH, and TOM GRAHAM. Large 4to, bound in buckram, 21s.

Murray (D. Christie), Novels by. Crown 8vo, cloth extra, 3s. 6d. each; post 8vo, illustrated boards, 2s. each.
A Life's Atonement.
A Model Father.
Joseph's Coat.
Coals of Fire.
By the Gate of the Sea.
Val Strange.
Hearts.

Crown 8vo, cloth extra, 3s. 6d. each.
The Way of the World.
A Bit of Human Nature.

North Italian Folk. By Mrs. COMYNS CARR. Illust. by RANDOLPH CALDECOTT. Square 8vo, cloth extra, 7s. 6d.

Number Nip (Stories about), the Spirit of the Giant Mountains. Retold for Children by WALTER GRAHAME. With Illustrations by J. MOYR SMITH. Post 8vo, cloth extra, 5s.

Nursery Hints: A Mother's Guide in Health and Disease. By N. E. DAVIES, L.R.C.P. Crown 8vo, 1s.; cloth, 1s. 6d.

Oliphant.—Whiteladies: A Novel. With Illustrations by ARTHUR HOPKINS and HENRY WOODS. Crown 8vo, cloth extra, 3s. 6d.; post 8vo, illustrated boards, 2s.

O'Connor.—Lord Beaconsfield A Biography. By T. P. O'CONNOR, M.P. Sixth Edition, with a New Preface, bringing the work down to the Death of Lord Beaconsfield. Crown 8vo, cloth extra, 7s. 6d.

O'Reilly.—Phœbe's Fortunes: A Novel. With Illustrations by HENRY TUCK. Post 8vo, illustrated boards, 2s.

O'Shaughnessy (Arth.), Works by:
Songs of a Worker. Fcap. 8vo, cloth extra, 7s. 6d.
Music and Moonlight. Fcap. 8vo, cloth extra, 7s. 6d.
Lays of France. Crown 8vo, cloth extra, 10s. 6d.

Ouida, Novels by. Crown 8vo, cloth extra, 5s. each; post 8vo, illustrated boards, 2s. each.

Held in Bondage.	Pascarel.
Strathmore.	Signa.
Chandos.	In a Winter City.
Under Two Flags.	Ariadne.
Cecil Castlemaine's Gage.	Friendship.
	Moths.
Idalia.	Pipistrello.
Tricotrin.	A Village Commune.
Puck.	
Folle Farine.	Bimbi.
Two Little Wooden Shoes.	In Maremma.
	Wanda.
A Dog of Flanders.	Frescoes.

Bimbi: PRESENTATION EDITION. Sq. 8vo, cloth gilt, cinnamon edges, 7s. 6d.

Princess Napraxine. New and Cheaper Edition. Crown 8vo, cloth extra, 5s.

Wisdom, Wit, and Pathos. Selected from the Works of OUIDA by F. SYDNEY MORRIS. Small crown 8vo, cloth extra, 5s.

Page (H. A.), Works by:
Thoreau: His Life and Aims: A Study. With a Portrait. Post 8vo, cloth limp, 2s. 6d.
Lights on the Way: Some Tales within a Tale. By the late J. H. ALEXANDER, B.A. Edited by H. A. PAGE Crown 8vo, cloth extra, 6s.

Pascal's Provincial Letters. A New Translation, with Historical Introduction and Notes, by T. M'CRIE, D.D. Post 8vo, cloth limp, 2s.

Patient's (The) Vade Mecum: How to get most Benefit from Medical Advice. By WILLIAM KNIGHT, M.R.C.S., and EDWARD KNIGHT, L.R.C.P. Crown 8vo, 1s.; cloth, 1s. 6d.

Paul Ferroll:
Post 8vo, illustrated boards, 2s. each.
Paul Ferroll: A Novel.
Why Paul Ferroll Killed his Wife.

Paul.—Gentle and Simple. By MARGARET AGNES PAUL. With a Frontispiece by HELEN PATERSON. Cr. 8vo, cloth extra, 3s. 6d.; post 8vo, illustrated boards, 2s.

Payn (James), Novels by.
Crown 8vo, cloth extra, 3s. 6d. each; post 8vo, illustrated boards, 2s. each.
Lost Sir Massingberd.
The Best of Husbands.
Walter's Word.
Halves. | Fallen Fortunes.
What He Cost Her.
Less Black than we're Painted.
By Proxy. | High Spirits.
Under One Roof. | Carlyon's Year.
A Confidential Agent.
Some Private Views.
A Grape from a Thorn.
For Cash Only. | From Exile.

Post 8vo, illustrated boards, 2s. each.
A Perfect Treasure.
Bentinck's Tutor.
Murphy's Master.
A County Family.
At Her Mercy.
A Woman's Vengeance.
Cecil's Tryst.
The Clyffards of Clyffe.
The Family Scapegrace.
The Foster Brothers.
Found Dead.
Gwendoline's Harvest.
Humorous Stories.
Like Father, Like Son.
A Marine Residence.
Married Beneath Him.
Mirk Abbey.
Not Wooed, but Won.
Two Hundred Pounds Reward.
Kit: A Memory.
The Canon's Ward.

In Peril and Privation: A Book for Boys. With numerous Illustrations. Crown 8vo, 6s. [*Preparing*.

Pennell (H. Cholmondeley), Works by: Post 8vo, cloth limp, 2s. 6d. each.
Puck on Pegasus. With Illustrations.
The Muses of Mayfair. Vers de Société, Selected and Edited by H. C. PENNELL.
Pegasus Re-Saddled. With Ten full-page Illusts. by G. DU MAURIER.

Phelps.—Beyond the Gates. By ELIZABETH STUART PHELPS, Author of "The Gates Ajar." Crown 8vo, cloth extra, 2s. 6d.

Pirkis (Mrs. C. L.) Novels by:
Trooping with Crows. Fcap. 8vo, picture cover, 1s.
Lady Lovelace. Three Vols., cr. 8vo, 31s. 6d.

Planche (J. R.), Works by:
The Cyclopædia of Costume; or, A Dictionary of Dress—Regal, Ecclesiastical, Civil, and Military—from the Earliest Period in England to the Reign of George the Third. Including Notices of Contemporaneous Fashions on the Continent, and a General History of the Costumes of the Principal Countries of Europe. Two Vols., demy 4to, half morocco profusely Illustrated with Coloured and Plain Plates and Woodcuts, £7 7s. The Vols. may also be had *separately* (each complete in itself) at £3 13s. 6d. each: Vol. I. THE DICTIONARY. Vol. II. A GENERAL HISTORY OF COSTUME IN EUROPE.
The Pursuivant of Arms; or, Heraldry Founded upon Facts. With Coloured Frontispiece and 200 Illustrations. Cr. 8vo, cloth extra, 7s. 6d.
Songs and Poems, from 1819 to 1879. Edited, with an Introduction, by his Daughter, Mrs. MACKARNESS. Crown 8vo, cloth extra, 6s.

Play-time: Sayings and Doings of Baby-land. By E. STANFORD. Large 4to, handsomely printed in Colours, 5s.

Plutarch's Lives of Illustrious Men. Translated from the Greek, with Notes Critical and Historical, and a Life of Plutarch, by JOHN and WILLIAM LANGHORNE. Two Vols., 8vo, cloth extra, with Portraits, 10s. 6d.

Poe (Edgar Allan):—
The Choice Works, in Prose and Poetry, of EDGAR ALLAN POE. With an Introductory Essay by CHARLES BAUDELAIRE, Portrait and Facsimiles. Crown 8vo, cl. extra, 7s. 6d.
The Mystery of Marie Roget, and other Stories. Post 8vo, illust.bds.,2s.

Pope's Poetical Works. Complete in One Vol. Post 8vo, cl. limp, 2s.

Power.—Philistia: A Novel. By CECIL POWER. Three Vols., cr. 8vo, 31s. 6d.

Price (E. C.), Novels by:
Crown 8vo, cloth extra, 3s. 6d.; post 8vo, illustrated boards, 2s.
Valentina. | The Foreigners.
Mrs. Lancaster's Rival.

Gerald. Three Vols., cr. 8vo, 31s. 6d.

Proctor (Richd. A.), Works by:
Flowers of the Sky. With 55 Illusts. Small crown 8vo, cloth extra, 4s. 6d.
Easy Star Lessons. With Star Maps for Every Night in the Year, Drawings of the Constellations, &c. Crown 8vo, cloth extra, 6s.
Familiar Science Studies. Crown 8vo, cloth extra, 7s. 6d.
Rough Ways made Smooth: A Series of Familiar Essays on Scientific Subjects. Cr. 8vo, cloth extra, 6s.
Our Place among Infinities: A Series of Essays contrasting our Little Abode in Space and Time with the Infinities Around us. Crown 8vo, cloth extra, 6s.
The Expanse of Heaven: A Series of Essays on the Wonders of the Firmament. Cr. 8vo, cloth extra, 6s.
Saturn and its System. New and Revised Edition, with 13 Steel Plates. Demy 8vo, cloth extra, 10s. 6d.
The Great Pyramid: Observatory, Tomb, and Temple. With Illustrations. Crown 8vo, cloth extra, 6s.
Mysteries of Time and Space. With Illusts. Cr. 8vo, cloth extra, 7s. 6d.
The Universe of Suns, and other Science Gleanings. With numerous Illusts. Cr. 8vo, cloth extra, 7s. 6d.
Wages and Wants of Science Workers. Crown 8vo, 1s. 6d.

Pyrotechnist's Treasury (The); or, Complete Art of Making Fireworks. By THOMAS KENTISH. With numerous Illustrations. Cr. 8vo, cl. extra, 4s. 6d.

Rabelais' Works. Faithfully Translated from the French, with variorum Notes, and numerous characteristic Illustrations by GUSTAVE DORÉ. Crown 8vo, cloth extra, 7s. 6d.

Rambosson.—Popular Astronomy. By J. RAMBOSSON, Laureate of the Institute of France. Translated by C. B. PITMAN. Crown 8vo, cloth gilt, with numerous Illustrations, and a beautifully executed Chart of Spectra, 7s. 6d.

Reader's Handbook (The) of Allusions, References, Plots, and Stories. By the Rev. Dr. BREWER. Fourth Edition, revised throughout, with a New Appendix, containing a COMPLETE ENGLISH BIBLIOGRAPHY. Cr. 8vo, 1,400 pages, cloth extra, 7s. 6d.

Richardson. — A Ministry of Health, and other Papers. By BENJAMIN WARD RICHARDSON, M.D., &c. Crown 8vo, cloth extra, 6s.

Reade (Charles, D.C.L.), Novels by. Post 8vo, illust., bds., 2s. each; or cr. 8vo, cl. ex., illust. 3s. 6d. each.
Peg Woffington. Illustrated by S. L. FILDES, A.R.A.
Christie Johnstone. Illustrated by WILLIAM SMALL.
It is Never Too Late to Mend. Illustrated by G. J. PINWELL.
The Course of True Love Never did run Smooth. Illustrated by HELEN PATERSON.
The Autobiography of a Thief; Jack of all Trades; and James Lambert. Illustrated by MATT STRETCH.
Love me Little, Love me Long. Illustrated by M. ELLEN EDWARDS.
The Double Marriage. Illust. by Sir JOHN GILBERT, R.A., and C. KEENE.
The Cloister and the Hearth. Illustrated by CHARLES KEENE.
Hard Cash. Illust. by F. W. LAWSON.
Griffith Gaunt. Illustrated by S. L. FILDES, A.R.A., and WM. SMALL.
Foul Play. Illust. by DU MAURIER.
Put Yourself in His Place. Illustrated by ROBERT BARNES.
A Terrible Temptation. Illustrated by EDW. HUGHES and A. W. COOPER.
The Wandering Heir. Illustrated by H. PATERSON, S. L. FILDES, A.R.A., C. GREEN, and H. WOODS, A.R.A.
A Simpleton. Illustrated by KATE CRAUFORD.
A Woman-Hater. Illustrated by THOS. COULDERY.
Readiana. With a Steel-plate Portrait of CHARLES READE.
Singleheart and Doubleface: A Matter-of-fact Romance. Illustrated by P. MACNAB.
Good Stories of Men and other Animals. Illustrated by E. A. ABBEY, PERCY MACQUOID, and JOSEPH NASH.
The Jilt, and other Stories. Illustrated by JOSEPH NASH.

Riddell (Mrs. J. H.), Novels by:
Crown 8vo, cloth extra, 3s. 6d. each; post 8vo, illustrated boards, 2s. each.
Her Mother's Darling.
The Prince of Wales's Garden Party.
Weird Stories.
The Uninhabited House.
Fairy Water.

Rimmer (Alfred), Works by:
Our Old Country Towns. With over 50 Illusts. Sq. 8vo, cloth gilt, 10s 6d.
Rambles Round Eton and Harrow. 50 Illusts. Sq. 8vo, cloth gilt, 10s. 6d.
About England with Dickens. With 58 Illusts. by ALFRED RIMMER and C. A. VANDERHOOF. Sq. 8vo, cl. gilt, 10s. 6d.

Robinson (F. W.), Novels by:
Crown 8vo, cloth extra. 3s. 6d.; post 8vo, illustrated boards, 2s.
   Women are Strange.
   The Hands of Justice.

Robinson (Phil), Works by:
   The Poets' Birds. Crown 8vo, cloth extra, 7s. 6d.
   The Poets' Beasts. Crown 8vo, cloth extra, 7s. 6d.   [*In the press.*

Robinson Crusoe: A beautiful reproduction of Major's Edition, with 37 Woodcuts and Two Steel Plates by GEORGE CRUIKSHANK, choicely printed. Crown 8vo, cloth extra, 7s. 6d. A few Large-Paper copies, printed on hand-made paper, with India proofs of the Illustrations, price 36s.

Rochefoucauld's Maxims and Moral Reflections. With Notes, and an Introductory Essay by SAINTE-BEUVE. Post 8vo, cloth limp, 2s.

Roll of Battle Abbey, The; or, A List of the Principal Warriors who came over from Normandy with William the Conqueror, and Settled in this Country, A.D. 1066-7. With the principal Arms emblazoned in Gold and Colours. Handsomely printed, 5s.

Rowley (Hon. Hugh), Works by:
Post 8vo, cloth limp, 2s. 6d. each.
   Puniana: Riddles and Jokes. With numerous Illustrations.
   More Puniana. Profusely Illustrated.

Russell (W. Clark), Works by:
   Round the Galley-Fire. Crown 8vo, cloth extra, 6s.; post 8vo, illustrated boards, 2s.
   On the Fo'k'sle Head: A Collection of Yarns and Sea Descriptions. Crown 8vo, cloth extra, 6s.

Sala.—Gaslight and Daylight. By GEORGE AUGUSTUS SALA. Post 8vo, illustrated boards, 2s.

Sanson.—Seven Generations of Executioners: Memoirs of the Sanson Family (1688 to 1847). Edited by HENRY SANSON. Cr.8vo,cl.ex. 3s. 6d.

Saunders (John), Novels by:
Crown 8vo, cloth extra, 3s. 6d. each; post 8vo, illustrated boards, 2s. each.
   Bound to the Wheel.
   One Against the World.
   Guy Waterman.
   The Lion in the Path.
   The Two Dreamers.

Saunders (Katharine), Novels by:
Crown 8vo, cloth extra, 3s. 6d. each; post 8vo, illustrated boards, 2s. each.
   Joan Merryweather.
   Margaret and Elizabeth.
   Gideon's Rock.
   The High Mills.

Crown 8vo, cloth extra, 3s. 6d. each.
   Heart Salvage. | Sebastian.

Science Gossip: An Illustrated Medium of Interchange for Students and Lovers of Nature. Edited by J. E. TAYLOR, F.L.S., &c. Devoted to Geology, Botany, Physiology, Chemistry, Zoology, Microscopy, Telescopy, Physiography, &c. Price 4d. Monthly; or 5s. per year, post free. Each Number contains a Coloured Plate and numerous Woodcuts. Vols. I. to XIV. may be had at 7s. 6d. each; and Vols. XV. to XX. (1884), at 5s. each. Cases for Binding, 1s. 6d. each.

Scott's (Sir Walter) Marmion. An entirely New Edition of this famous and popular Poem, with over 100 new Illustrations by leading Artists. Elegantly and appropriately bound, small 4to, cloth extra, 16s.

[The immediate success of "The Lady of the Lake," published in 1882, has encouraged Messrs. CHATTO and WINDUS to bring out a Companion Edition of this not less popular and famous poem. Produced in the same form, and with the same careful and elaborate style of illustration, regardless of cost, Mr. Anthony's skilful supervision is sufficient guarantee that the work is elegant and tasteful as well as correct.]

"Secret Out" Series, The. Crown 8vo, cloth extra, profusely Illustrated, 4s. 6d. each.
   The Secret Out: One Thousand Tricks with Cards, and other Recreations; with Entertaining Experiments in Drawing-room or "White Magic." By W. H. CREMER. 300 Engravings.
   The Pyrotechnist's Treasury; or, Complete Art of Making Fireworks. By THOMAS KENTISH. With numerous Illustrations.
   The Art of Amusing: A Collection of Graceful Arts, Games, Tricks, Puzzles, and Charades. By FRANK BELLEW. With 300 Illustrations.
   Hanky-Panky: Very Easy Tricks, Very Difficult Tricks, White Magic, Sleight of Hand. Edited by W. H. CREMER. With 200 Illustrations.

"Secret Out" Series, continued—
  The Merry Circle: A Book of New Intellectual Games and Amusements. By Clara Bellew. With many Illustrations.
  Magician's Own Book: Performances with Cups and Balls, Eggs, Hats, Handkerchiefs, &c. All from actual Experience. Edited by W. H. Cremer. 200 Illustrations.
  Magic No Mystery: Tricks with Cards, Dice, Balls, &c., with fully descriptive Directions; the Art of Secret Writing; Training of Performing Animals, &c. With Coloured Frontis. and many Illusts.

Senior (William), Works by:
  Travel and Trout in the Antipodes. Crown 8vo, cloth extra, 6s.
  By Stream and Sea. Post 8vo, cloth limp, 2s. 6d.

Seven Sagas (The) of Prehistoric Man. By James H. Stoddart, Author of "The Village Life." Crown 8vo, cloth extra, 6s.

Shakespeare:
  The First Folio Shakespeare.—Mr. William Shakespeare's Comedies, Histories, and Tragedies. Published according to the true Originall Copies. London, Printed by Isaac Iaggard and Ed. Blount. 1623.—A Reproduction of the extremely rare original, in reduced facsimile, by a photographic process—ensuring the strictest accuracy in every detail. Small 8vo, half-Roxburghe, 7s. 6d.
  The Lansdowne Shakespeare. Beautifully printed in red and black, in small but very clear type. With engraved facsimile of Droeshout's Portrait. Post 8vo, cloth extra, 7s. 6d.
  Shakespeare for Children: Tales from Shakespeare. By Charles and Mary Lamb. With numerous Illustrations, coloured and plain, by J. Moyr Smith. Cr 4to, cl. gilt, 6s.
  The Handbook of Shakespeare Music. Being an Account of 350 Pieces of Music, set to Words taken from the Plays and Poems of Shakespeare, the compositions ranging from the Elizabethan Age to the Present Time. By Alfred Roffe. 4to, half-Roxburghe, 7s.
  A Study of Shakespeare. By Algernon Charles Swinburne. Crown 8vo, cloth extra, 8s.
  The Dramatic Works of Shakespeare: The Text of the First Edition, carefully reprinted. Eight Vols., demy 8vo, cloth boards, 40s.
  *** Only 250 Sets have been printed, each one numbered. The volumes will not be sold separately.

Shelley's Complete Works, in Four Vols., post 8vo, cloth limp, 8s.; or separately, 2s. each. Vol. I. contains his Early Poems, Queen Mab, &c., with an Introduction by Leigh Hunt; Vol. II., his Later Poems, Laon and Cythna, &c.; Vol. III., Posthumous Poems, the Shelley Papers, &c.: Vol. IV., his Prose Works, including A Refutation of Deism, Zastrozzi, St. Irvyne, &c.

Sheridan:—
  Sheridan's Complete Works, with Life and Anecdotes. Including his Dramatic Writings, printed from the Original Editions, his Works in Prose and Poetry, Translations, Speeches, Jokes, Puns, &c. With a Collection of Sheridaniana. Crown 8vo, cloth extra, gilt, with 10 full-page Tinted Illustrations, 7s. 6d.
  Sheridan's Comedies: The Rivals, and The School for Scandal. Edited, with an Introduction and Notes to each Play, and a Biographical Sketch of Sheridan, by Brander Matthews. With Decorative Vignettes and 10 full-page Illustrations. Demy 8vo, half-parchment, 12s. 6d.

Short Sayings of Great Men. With Historical and Explanatory Notes by Samuel A. Bent, M.A. Demy 8vo, cloth extra, 7s. 6d.

Sidney's (Sir Philip) Complete Poetical Works, including all those in "Arcadia." With Portrait, Memorial-Introduction, Essay on the Poetry of Sidney, and Notes, by the Rev. A. B. Grosart, D.D. Three Vols., crown 8vo, cloth boards, 18s.

Signboards: Their History. With Anecdotes of Famous Taverns and Remarkable Characters. By Jacob Larwood and John Camden Hotten. Crown 8vo, cloth extra, with 100 Illustrations, 7s. 6d.

Sims (G. R.)—How the Poor Live. With 60 Illustrations by Fred. Barnard. Large 4to, 1s.

Sketchley.—A Match in the Dark. By Arthur Sketchley. Post 8vo, illustrated boards, 2s.

Slang Dictionary, The: Etymological, Historical, and Anecdotal. Crown 8vo, cloth extra, gilt, 6s. 6d.

Smith (J. Moyr), Works by:
  The Prince of Argolis: A Story of the Old Greek Fairy Time. By J. Moyr Smith. Small 8vo, cloth extra, with 130 Illustrations, 3s. 6d.

Smith's (J. Moyr) Works, *continued*—
Tales of Old Thule. Collected and Illustrated by J. Moyr Smith. Cr. 8vo, cloth gilt, profusely Illust., 6s.
The Wooing of the Water Witch: A Northern Oddity. By Evan Daldorne. Illustrated by J. Moyr Smith. Small 8vo, cloth extra, 6s.

Society in London. By a Foreign Resident. Fourth Edition. Crown 8vo, cloth extra, 6s.

Spalding.—Elizabethan Demonology: An Essay in Illustration of the Belief in the Existence of Devils, and the Powers possessed by Them. By T. Alfred Spalding, LL.B. Crown 8vo, cloth extra, 5s.

Spanish Legendary Tales. By S. G. E. Middlemore, Author of "Round a Posado Fire." Crown 8vo, cloth extra, 6s. [*In the press.*

Speight.—The Mysteries of Heron Dyke. By T. W. Speight. With a Frontispiece by M. Ellen Edwards. Crown 8vo, cloth extra, 3s. 6d.; post 8vo, illustrated boards, 2s.

Spenser for Children. By M. H. Towry. With Illustrations by Walter J Morgan. Crown 4to, with Coloured Illustrations, cloth gilt, 6s.

Staunton.—Laws and Practice of Chess; Together with an Analysis of the Openings, and a Treatise on End Games. By Howard Staunton. Edited by Robert B. Wormald. New Edition, small cr. 8vo, cloth extra, 5s.

Sterndale.—The Afghan Knife: A Novel. By Robert Armitage Sterndale. Cr. 8vo, cloth extra, 3s. 6d.; post 8vo, illustrated boards, 2s.

Stevenson (R. Louis), Works by:
Travels with a Donkey in the Cevennes. Frontispiece by Walter Crane. Post 8vo, cloth limp, 2s. 6d.
An Inland Voyage. With Front, by W. Crane. Post 8vo, cl. lp., 2s. 6d.
Virginibus Puerisque, and other Papers. Crown 8vo, cloth extra, 6s.
Familiar Studies of Men and Books. Crown 8vo, cloth extra, 6s.
New Arabian Nights. Crown 8vo, cl. extra, 6s.; post 8vo, illust. bds., 2s.
The Silverado Squatters. With Frontispiece. Cr. 8vo, cloth extra, 6s.
Prince Otto: A Romance. Crown 8vo, cloth extra, 6s. [*In preparation.*

St. John.—A Levantine Family. By Bayle St. John, Post 8vo, illustrated boards, 2s.

Stoddard.—Summer Cruising in the South Seas. By Charles Warren Stoddard. Illust. by Wallis Mackay. Crown 8vo, cl. extra, 3s. 6d.

St. Pierre.—Paul and Virginia, and The Indian Cottage. By Bernardin St. Pierre. Edited, with Life, by Rev. E. Clarke. Post 8vo, cl. lp., 2s.

Stories from Foreign Novelists. With Notices of their Lives and Writings. By Helen and Alice Zimmern; and a Frontispiece. Crown 8vo, cloth extra, 3s. 6d.

Strutt's Sports and Pastimes of the People of England; including the Rural and Domestic Recreations, May Games, Mummeries, Shows, Processions, Pageants, and Pompous Spectacles, from the Earliest Period to the Present Time. With 140 Illustrations. Edited by William Hone. Crown 8vo, cloth extra, 7s. 6d.

Suburban Homes (The) of London: A Residential Guide to Favourite London Localities, their Society, Celebrities, and Associations. With Notes on their Rental, Rates, and House Accommodation. With Map of Suburban London. Cr. 8vo, cl. ex., 7s. 6d.

Swift's Choice Works, in Prose and Verse. With Memoir, Portrait, and Facsimiles of the Maps in the Original Edition of "Gulliver's Travels." Cr. 8vo, cloth extra, 7s. 6d.

Swinburne (Algernon C.), Works by:
The Queen Mother and Rosamond. Fcap. 8vo, 5s.
Atalanta in Calydon. Crown 8vo, 6s.
Chastelard. A Tragedy. Cr. 8vo, 7s.
Poems and Ballads. First Series. Fcap. 8vo, 9s. Also in crown 8vo, at same price.
Poems and Ballads. Second Series. Fcap. 8vo, 9s. Cr. 8vo, same price.
Notes on Poems and Reviews. 8vo, 1s.
William Blake: A Critical Essay. With Facsimile Paintings. Demy 8vo, 16s.
Songs before Sunrise. Cr. 8vo, 10s. 6d.
Bothwell: A Tragedy. Cr. 8vo, 12s. 6d.
George Chapman: An Essay. Crown 8vo, 7s.
Songs of Two Nations. Cr. 8vo, 6s.
Essays and Studies. Crown 8vo, 12s.
Erechtheus: A Tragedy. Cr. 8vo, 6s.
Note of an English Republican on the Muscovite Crusade. 8vo, 1s.
A Note on Charlotte Bronte. Crown 8vo, 6s.
A Study of Shakespeare. Cr. 8vo, 6s.
Songs of the Springtides. Cr. 8vo, 6s.
Studies in Song. Crown 8vo, 7s.

SWINBURNE (ALGERNON C.) WORKS, *con.*
Mary Stuart: A Tragedy. Cr. 8vo, 8s.
Tristram of Lyonesse, and other Poems. Crown 8vo, 9s.
A Century of Roundels. Small 4to, cloth extra, 8s.
A Midsummer Holiday, and other Poems. Crown 8vo, cloth extra, 7s.
Marino Faliero: A Tragedy. **Crown** 8vo, cloth extra, 6s.

Symonds.—Wine, Women and Song: Mediæval Latin Students' Songs. Now first translated into English Verse, with an Essay by J. ADDINGTON SYMONDS. Small 8vo, parchment, 6s.

Syntax's (Dr.) Three Tours: In Search of the Picturesque, in Search of Consolation, and in Search of a Wife. With the whole of ROWLANDSON'S droll page Illustrations in Colours and a Life of the Author by J. C. HOTTEN. Med. 8vo, cloth extra, 7s. 6d.

Taine's History of English Literature. Translated by HENRY VAN LAUN. Four Vols., small 8vo, cloth boards, 30s.—POPULAR EDITION, Two Vols., crown 8vo, cloth extra, 15s.

Taylor (Dr. J. E., F.L.S.), Works by:
The Sagacity and Morality of Plants: A Sketch of the Life and Conduct of the Vegetable Kingdom. With Coloured Frontispiece and 100 Illusts. Crown 8vo, cl. extra, 7s. 6d.
Our Common British Fossils, and Where to Find Them. With numerous Illustrations. **Crown 8vo**, cloth extra, 7s. 6d.

Taylor's (Bayard) Diversions of the Echo Club: Burlesques of Modern Writers. Post 8vo, cl. limp, 2s.

Taylor's (Tom) Historical Dramas: "Clancarty," "Jeanne Darc," "'Twixt Axe and Crown," "The Fool's Revenge," "Arkwright's Wife," "Anne Boleyn," "Plot and Passion." One Vol., crown 8vo, cloth extra, 7s. 6d.
*** The Plays may also be had separately, at 1s. each.

Tennyson (Lord): A Biographical Sketch. By H. J. JENNINGS. With a Photograph-Portrait. **Crown** 8vo, cloth extra, 6s.

Thackerayana: Notes and Anecdotes. Illustrated by Hundreds of Sketches by WILLIAM MAKEPEACE THACKERAY, depicting Humorous Incidents in his School-life, and Favourite Characters in the books of his every-day reading. With Coloured Frontispiece. Cr. 8vo, cl. extra, 7s. 6d.

Thomas (Bertha), Novels by. Crown 8vo, cloth extra, 3s. 6d. each post 8vo, illustrated boards, 2s. each.
Cressida.
Proud Maisie
The Violin-Player.

Thomas (M.).—A Fight for Life: A Novel. By W. MOY THOMAS. Post 8vo, illustrated boards, 2s.

Thomson's Seasons and Castle of Indolence. With a Biographical and Critical Introduction by ALLAN CUNNINGHAM, and over 50 fine Illustrations on Steel and Wood. Crown 8vo, cloth extra, gilt edges, 7s. 6d.

Thornbury (Walter), Works by
Haunted London. Edited by EDWARD WALFORD, M.A. With Illustrations by F. W. FAIRHOLT, F.S.A. Crown 8vo, cloth extra, 7s. 6d.
The Life and Correspondence of J. M. W. Turner. Founded upon Letters and Papers furnished by his Friends and fellow Academicians. With numerous Illusts. in Colours, facsimiled from Turner's Original Drawings. Cr. 8vo, cl. extra, 7s. 6d.
Old Stories Re-told. Post 8vo, cloth limp, 2s. 6d.
Tales for the Marines. Post 8vo, illustrated boards, 2s.

Timbs (John), Works by:
The History of Clubs and Club Life in London. With Anecdotes of its Famous Coffee-houses, Hostelries, and Taverns. With numerous Illustrations. Cr. 8vo, cloth extra, 7s. 6d.
English Eccentrics and Eccentricities: Stories of Wealth and Fashion, Delusions, Impostures, and Fanatic Missions, Strange Sights and Sporting Scenes, Eccentric Artists, Theatrical Folks, Men of Letters, &c. With nearly 50 Illusts. Crown 8vo, cloth extra, 7s. 6d.

Torrens. — The Marquess Wellesley, Architect of Empire. An Historic Portrait. By W. M. TORRENS, M.P. Demy 8vo, cloth extra, 14s.

Trollope (Anthony), Novels by:
Crown 8vo, cloth extra, 3s. 6d. each post 8vo, illustrated boards, 2s. each.
The Way We Live Now.
The American Senator.
Kept in the Dark.
Frau Frohmann.
Marion Fay.
Mr. Scarborough's Family.
The Land-Leaguers.

Post 8vo, illustrated boards, 2s. each.
The Golden Lion of Granpere.
John Caldigate.

Trollope (Frances E.), Novels by
Crown 8vo, cloth extra, 3s. 6d.; post 8vo, illustrated boards, 2s.
  Like Ships upon the Sea.
  Mabel's Progress.
  Anne Furness.

Trollope (T. A.).—Diamond Cut Diamond, and other Stories. By T. ADOLPHUS TROLLOPE. Cr. 8vo, cl. ex., 3s. 6d.; post 8vo, illust. boards, 2s.

Trowbridge.—Farnell's Folly: A Novel. By J. T. TROWBRIDGE. Two Vols., crown 8vo, 12s.

Turgenieff (Ivan), &c. Stories from Foreign Novelists. Post 8vo, illustrated boards, 2s.

Tytler (Sarah), Novels by:
Crown 8vo, cloth extra, 3s. 6d. each; post 8vo, illustrated boards, 2s. each.
  What She Came Through.
  The Bride's Pass.

  Saint Mungo's City. Crown 8vo, cloth extra, 3s. 6d.
  Beauty and the Beast. Three Vols., crown 8vo, 31s. 6d.

Tytler (C. C. Fraser-).—Mistress Judith: A Novel. By C. C. FRASER-TYTLER. Cr. 8vo, cloth extra, 3s. 6d.; post 8vo, illust. boards, 2s.

Van Laun.—History of French Literature. By HENRY VAN LAUN. Complete in Three Vols., demy 8vo, cloth boards, 7s. 6d. each.

Villari.—A Double Bond: A Story. By LINDA VILLARI. Fcap. 8vo, picture cover, 1s.

Walcott.—Church Work and Life in English Minsters; and the English Student's Monasticon. By the Rev. MACKENZIE E. C. WALCOTT, B.D. Two Vols., crown 8vo, cloth extra, with Map and Ground-Plans, 14s.

Walford (Edw., M.A.), Works by:
The County Families of the United Kingdom. Containing Notices of the Descent, Birth, Marriage, Education, &c., of more than 12,000 distinguished Heads of Families, their Heirs Apparent or Presumptive, the Offices they hold or have held, their Town and Country Addresses, Clubs, &c. Twenty-fifth Annual Edition, for 1885, cloth, full gilt, 50s.

The Shilling Peerage (1885). Containing an Alphabetical List of the House of Lords, Dates of Creation, Lists of Scotch and Irish Peers, Addresses, &c. 32mo, cloth, 1s. Published annually.

WALFORD'S (EDW., M.A.) WORKS, con.—
The Shilling Baronetage (1885). Containing an Alphabetical List of the Baronets of the United Kingdom, short Biographical Notices, Dates of Creation, Addresses, &c. 32mo, cloth, 1s. Published annually.

The Shilling Knightage (1885). Containing an Alphabetical List of the Knights of the United Kingdom, short Biographical Notices, Dates of Creation, Addresses, &c. 32mo, cloth, 1s. Published annually.

The Shilling House of Commons (1885). Containing a List of all the Members of the British Parliament, their Town and Country Addresses, &c. 32mo, cloth, 1s. Published annually.

The Complete Peerage, Baronetage, Knightage, and House of Commons (1885). In One Volume, royal 32mo, cloth extra, gilt edges, 5s. Published annually.

Haunted London. By WALTER THORNBURY. Edited by EDWARD WALFORD, M.A. With Illustrations by F. W. FAIRHOLT, F S.A. Crown 8vo, cloth extra, 7s. 6d.

Walton and Cotton's Complete Angler; or, The Contemplative Man's Recreation; being a Discourse of Rivers, Fishponds, Fish and Fishing, written by IZAAK WALTON; and Instructions how to Angle for a Trout or Grayling in a clear Stream, by CHARLES COTTON. With Original Memoirs and Notes by Sir HARRIS NICOLAS, and 61 Copperplate Illustrations. Large crown 8vo, cloth antique, 7s. 6d.

Wanderer's Library, The:
Crown 8vo, cloth extra, 3s. 6d. each.
Wanderings in Patagonia; or, Life among the Ostrich Hunters. By JULIUS BEERBOHM. Illustrated.
Camp Notes: Stories of Sport and Adventure in Asia, Africa, and America. By FREDERICK BOYLE.
Savage Life. By FREDERICK BOYLE.
Merrie England in the Olden Time. By GEORGE DANIEL. With Illustrations by ROBT. CRUIKSHANK.
Circus Life and Circus Celebrities. By THOMAS FROST.
The Lives of the Conjurers. By THOMAS FROST.
The Old Showmen and the Old London Fairs. By THOMAS FROST.
Low-Life Deeps. An Account of the Strange Fish to be found there. By JAMES GREENWOOD.
The Wilds of London. By JAMES GREENWOOD.
Tunis: The Land and the People. By the Chevalier de HESSE-WARTEGG. With 22 Illustrations.

WANDERER'S LIBRARY, THE, continued—
  The Life and Adventures of a Cheap Jack. By One of the Fraternity. Edited by CHARLES HINDLEY.
  The World Behind the Scenes. By PERCY FITZGERALD.
  Tavern Anecdotes and Sayings: Including the Origin of Signs, and Reminiscences connected with Taverns, Coffee Houses, Clubs, &c. By CHARLES HINDLEY. With Illusts.
  The Genial Showman: Life and Adventures of Artemus Ward. By E. P. HINGSTON. With a Frontispiece.
  The Story of the London Parks. By JACOB LARWOOD. With Illusts.
  London Characters. By HENRY MAYHEW. Illustrated.
  Seven Generations of Executioners: Memoirs of the Sanson Family (1688 to 1847). Edited by HENRY SANSON.
  Summer Cruising in the South Seas. By C. WARREN STODDARD. Illustrated by WALLIS MACKAY.

Warner.—A Roundabout Journey. By CHARLES DUDLEY WARNER, Author of "My Summer in a Garden." Crown 8vo, cloth extra, 6s.

Warrants, &c.:—
  Warrant to Execute Charles I. An exact Facsimile, with the Fifty-nine Signatures, and corresponding Seals. Carefully printed on paper to imitate the Original, 22 in. by 14 in. Price 2s.
  Warrant to Execute Mary Queen of Scots. An exact Facsimile, including the Signature of Queen Elizabeth, and a Facsimile of the Great Seal. Beautifully printed on paper to imitate the Original MS. Price 2s.
  Magna Charta. An exact Facsimile of the Original Document in the British Museum, printed on fine plate paper, nearly 3 feet long by 2 feet wide, with the Arms and Seals emblazoned in Gold and Colours. Price 5s.
  The Roll of Battle Abbey; or, A List of the Principal Warriors who came over from Normandy with William the Conqueror, and Settled in this Country, A.D. 1066-7. With the principal Arms emblazoned in Gold and Colours. Price 5s.

Weather, How to Foretell the, with the Pocket Spectroscope. By F. W. CORY, M.R.C.S. Eng., F.R.Met. Soc., &c. With 10 Illustrations. Crown 8vo, 1s.; cloth, 1s. 6d.

Westropp.—Handbook of Pottery and Porcelain; or, History of those Arts from the Earliest Period. By HODDER M. WESTROPP. With numerous Illustrations, and a List of Marks. Crown 8vo, cloth limp, 4s. 6d.

Whistler v. Ruskin: Art and Art Critics. By J. A. MACNEILL WHISTLER. 7th Edition, sq. 8vo, 1s.

White's Natural History of Selborne. Edited, with Additions, by THOMAS BROWN, F.L.S. Post 8vo, cloth limp, 2s.

Williams (W. Mattieu, F.R.A.S.), Works by:
  Science Notes. See the GENTLEMAN'S MAGAZINE. 1s. Monthly.
  Science in Short Chapters. Crown 8vo, cloth extra, 7s. 6d.
  A Simple Treatise on Heat. Crown 8vo, cloth limp, with Illusts., 2s. 6d.
  The Chemistry of Cookery. Crown 8vo, cloth extra, 6s.

Wilson (Dr. Andrew, F.R.S.E.), Works by:
  Chapters on Evolution: A Popular History of the Darwinian and Allied Theories of Development. Second Edition. Crown 8vo, cloth extra, with 259 Illustrations, 7s. 6d.
  Leaves from a Naturalist's Notebook. Post 8vo, cloth limp, 2s. 6d.
  Leisure-Time Studies, chiefly Biological. Third Edition, with a New Preface. Crown 8vo, cloth extra, with Illustrations, 6s.

Winter (J. S.), Stories by:
  Crown 8vo, cloth extra, 3s. 6d. each; post 8vo, illustrated boards, 2s. each.
  Cavalry Life. | Regimental Legends.

Women of the Day: A Biographical Dictionary of Notable Contemporaries. By FRANCES HAYS. Crown 8vo, cloth extra, 5s.

Wood.—Sabina: A Novel. By Lady WOOD. Post 8vo, illust. bds., 2s.

Words, Facts, and Phrases: A Dictionary of Curious, Quaint, and Out-of-the-Way Matters. By ELIEZER EDWARDS. New and cheaper issue, cr. 8vo, cl. ex., 7s. 6d.; half-bound, 9s.

Wright (Thomas), Works by:
  Caricature History of the Georges. (The House of Hanover.) With 400 Pictures, Caricatures, Squibs, Broadsides, Window Pictures, &c. Crown 8vo, cloth extra, 7s. 6d.
  History of Caricature and of the Grotesque in Art, Literature, Sculpture, and Painting. Profusely Illustrated by F. W. FAIRHOLT, F.S.A. Large post 8vo, cl. ex., 7s. 6d.

Yates (Edmund), Novels by:
  Post 8vo, illustrated boards, 2s. each.
  Castaway. | The Forlorn Hope.
  Land at Last.

NOVELS BY THE BEST AUTHORS.

WILKIE COLLINS'S NEW NOVEL.
"I Say No." By WILKIE COLLINS. Three Vols., crown 8vo.

Mrs. CASHEL HOEY'S NEW NOVEL.
The Lover's Creed. By Mrs. CASHEL HOEY, Author of "The Blossoming of an Aloe," &c. With 12 Illustrations by P. MACNAB. Three Vols., cr. 8vo.

SARAH TYTLER'S NEW NOVEL.
Beauty and the Beast. By SARAH TYTLER, Author of "The Bride's Pass," "Saint Mungo's City," "Citoyenne Jacqueline," &c. Three Vols., cr. 8vo.

NEW NOVELS BY CHAS. GIBBON.
By Mead and Stream. By CHARLES GIBBON, Author of "Robin Gray," "The Golden Shaft," "Queen of the Meadow," &c. Three Vols., cr. 8vo.

A Hard Knot. By CHARLES GIBBON. Three Vols., crown 8vo.

Heart's Delight. By CHARLES GIBBON. Three Vols., crown 8vo. [*Shortly.*

NEW NOVEL BY CECIL POWER.
Philistia. By CECIL POWER. Three Vols., crown 8vo.

NEW NOVEL BY THE AUTHOR OF "VALENTINA."
Gerald. By ELEANOR C. PRICE. Three Vols., crown 8vo.

BASIL'S NEW NOVEL.
"The Wearing of the Green." By BASIL, Author of "Love the Debt," "A Drawn Game," &c. Three Vols., crown 8vo.

NEW NOVEL BY J. T. TROWBRIDGE.
Farnell's Folly. Two **Vols., crown 8vo,** 12s.

Mrs. PIRKIS' NEW NOVEL.
Lady Lovelace. By C. L. PIRKIS, Author of "A Very Opal." Three Vols., crown 8vo.

THE PICCADILLY NOVELS.
Popular Stories by the Best Authors. LIBRARY EDITIONS, many Illustrated, crown 8vo, cloth extra, 3s. 6d. each.

BY MRS. ALEXANDER.
Maid, Wife, or Widow?

BY BASIL.
A Drawn Game.

BY W. BESANT & JAMES RICE.
Ready-Money Mortiboy.
My Little Girl.
The Case of Mr. Lucraft.
This Son of Vulcan.
With Harp and Crown.
The Golden Butterfly.
By Celia's Arbour.
The Monks of Thelema.
'Twas in Trafalgar's Bay.
The Seamy Side.
The Ten Years' Tenant.
The Chaplain of the Fleet.
Dorothy Forster.

BY WALTER BESANT.
All Sorts and Conditions of Men.
The Captains' Room.
All in a Garden Fair.
Dorothy Forster.

BY ROBERT BUCHANAN.
A Child of Nature.
God and the Man.
The Shadow of the Sword.
The Martyrdom of Madeline.
Love Me for Ever.
Annan Water. | The New Abelard.
Matt. | Foxglove Manor.

BY MRS. H. LOVETT CAMERON.
Deceivers Ever. | Juliet's Guardian.

BY MORTIMER COLLINS.
Sweet Anne Page.
Transmigration.
From Midnight to Midnight.

MORTIMER & FRANCES COLLINS.
Blacksmith and Scholar.
The Village Comedy.
You Play me False.

BY WILKIE COLLINS.
Antonina. | New Magdalen.
Basil. | The Frozen Deep.
Hide and Seek. | The Law and the
The Dead Secret. | Lady.
Queen of Hearts. | The Two Destinies
My Miscellanies. | Haunted Hotel.
Woman in White. | The Fallen Leaves
The Moonstone. | Jezebel's Daughter
Man and Wife. | The Black Robe.
Poor Miss Finch. | Heart and Science
Miss or Mrs.?

BY DUTTON COOK.
Paul Foster's Daughter.

BY WILLIAM CYPLES.
Hearts of Gold.

BY ALPHONSE DAUDET.
Port Salvation.

BY JAMES DE MILLE.
A Castle in Spain.

BOOKS PUBLISHED BY

PICCADILLY NOVELS, continued—
BY J. LEITH DERWENT.
Our Lady of Tears. | Circe's Lovers.
BY M. BETHAM-EDWARDS.
Felicia. | Kitty.
BY MRS. ANNIE EDWARDES.
Archie Lovell.
BY R. E. FRANCILLON.
Olympia. | One by One.
Queen Cophetua. | A Real Queen.
Prefaced by Sir BARTLE FRERE.
Pandurang Hari.
BY EDWARD GARRETT.
The Capel Girls.
BY CHARLES GIBBON.
Robin Gray. | For Lack of Gold.
In Love and War.
What will the World Say?
For the King.
In Honour Bound.
Queen of the Meadow.
In Pastures Green.
The Flower of the Forest.
A Heart's Problem.
The Braes of Yarrow.
The Golden Shaft.
Of High Degree.
Fancy Free. | Loving a Dream.
BY HALL CAINE.
The Shadow of a Crime.
BY THOMAS HARDY.
Under the Greenwood Tree.
BY JULIAN HAWTHORNE.
Garth.
Ellice Quentin.
Sebastian Strome.
Prince Saroni's Wife.
Dust. | Fortune's Fool.
Beatrix Randolph.
Miss Cadogna.
BY SIR A. HELPS.
Ivan de Biron.
BY MRS. ALFRED HUNT.
Thornicroft's Model
The Leaden Casket.
Self Condemned.
BY JEAN INGELOW.
Fated to be Free.
BY HARRIETT JAY.
The Queen of Connaught
The Dark Colleen.
BY HENRY KINGSLEY.
Number Seventeen.
Oakshott Castle

PICCADILLY NOVELS, continued—
BY E LYNN LINTON.
Patricia Kemball.
Atonement of Leam Dundas.
The World Well Lost.
Under which Lord?
With a Silken Thread.
The Rebel of the Family
"My Love!" | Ione.
BY HENRY W. LUCY.
Gideon Fleyce.
BY JUSTIN McCARTHY, M.P
The Waterdale Neighbours.
My Enemy's Daughter.
Linley Rochford. | A Fair Saxon.
Dear Lady Disdain.
Miss Misanthrope.
Donna Quixote.
The Comet of a Season.
Maid of Athens.
BY GEORGE MAC DONALD, LL.D.
Paul Faber, Surgeon.
Thomas Wingfold, Curate.
BY MRS. MACDONELL.
Quaker Cousins.
BY KATHARINE S. MACQUOID.
Lost Rose | The Evil Eye.
BY FLORENCE MARRYAT.
Open! Sesame! | Written in Fire.
BY JEAN MIDDLEMASS.
Touch and Go.
BY D. CHRISTIE MURRAY.
Life's Atonement. | Coals of Fire.
Joseph's Coat. | Val Strange.
A Model Father. | Hearts.
By the Gate of the Sea
The Way of the World.
A Bit of Human Nature.
BY MRS. OLIPHANT.
Whiteladies.
BY MARGARET A. PAUL.
Gentle and Simple.
BY JAMES PAYN.
Lost Sir Massingberd. | Carlyon's Year.
Best of Husbands | A Confidential Agent.
Fallen Fortunes. | From Exile.
Halves. | A Grape from a Thorn.
Walter's Word.
What He Cost Her | For Cash Only.
Less Black than We're Painted. | Some Private Views.
By Proxy.
High Spirits. | Kit: A Memory.
Under One Roof. | The Canon's Ward.
BY E. C. PRICE.
Valentina. | The Foreigners.
Mrs. Lancaster's Rival.

PICCADILLY NOVELS, *continued—*
BY CHARLES READE, D.C.L.
It Is Never Too Late to Mend.
Hard Cash. | Peg Woffington.
Christie Johnstone.
Griffith Gaunt. | Foul Play.
The Double Marriage.
Love Me Little, Love Me Long.
The Cloister and the Hearth.
The Course of True Love.
The Autobiography of a Thief.
Put Yourself In His Place.
A Terrible Temptation.
The Wandering Heir. | A Simpleton.
A Woman-Hater. | Readiana.
Singleheart and Doubleface.
The Jilt. [mals.
Good Stories of Men and other Ani-
BY MRS. J. H. RIDDELL.
Her Mother's Darling.
Prince of Wales's Garden-Party.
Weird Stories.
BY F. W. ROBINSON.
Women are Strange.
The Hands of Justice.
BY JOHN SAUNDERS.
Bound to the Wheel.
Guy Waterman. | Two Dreamers.
One Against the World.
The Lion in the Path.
BY KATHARINE SAUNDERS.
Joan Merryweather.
Margaret and Elizabeth.
Gideon's Rock. | Heart Salvage.
The High Mills. | Sebastian.

PICCADILLY NOVELS, *continued—*
BY T. W SPEIGHT.
The Mysteries of Heron Dyke.
BY R. A. STERNDALE.
The Afghan Knife.
BY BERTHA THOMAS.
Proud Maisie. | Cressida.
The Violin-Player.
BY ANTHONY TROLLOPE.
The Way we Live Now.
The American Senator
Frau Frohmann. | Marion Fay.
Kept in the Dark.
Mr. Scarborough's Family.
The Land-Leaguers.
BY FRANCES E. TROLLOPE.
Like Ships upon the Sea.
Anne Furness.
Mabel's Progress.
BY T. A. TROLLOPE.
Diamond Cut Diamond
By IVAN TURGENIEFF and Others.
Stories from Foreign Novelists.
BY SARAH TYTLER.
What She Came Through.
The Bride's Pass.
Saint Mungo's City.
BY C. C. FRASER-TYTLER.
Mistress Judith.
BY J. S. WINTER.
Cavalry Life.
Regimental Legends.

CHEAP EDITIONS OF POPULAR NOVELS.
Post 8vo, illustrated boards, 2s. each.

BY EDMOND ABOUT.
The Fellah.
BY HAMILTON AÏDÉ.
Carr of Carrlyon. | Confidences
BY MRS. ALEXANDER.
Maid, Wife, or Widow?
Valerie's Fate.
BY SHELSLEY BEAUCHAMP.
Grantley Grange.
BY W. BESANT & JAMES RICE
Ready-Money Mortiboy.
With Harp and Crown.
This Son of Vulcan. | My Little Girl.
The Case of Mr. Lucraft.
The Golden Butterfly.
By Celia's Arbour.
The Monks of Thelema.

BY BESANT AND RICE, *continued—*
'Twas in Trafalgar's Bay.
The Seamy Side.
The Ten Years' Tenant.
The Chaplain of the Fleet.
BY WALTER BESANT.
All Sorts and Conditions of Men.
The Captains' Room.
All In a Garden Fair.
BY FREDERICK BOYLE.
Camp Notes. | Savage Life.
Chronicles of No-man's Land.
BY BRET HARTE.
An Heiress of Red Dog.
The Luck of Roaring Camp.
Californian Stories.
Gabriel Conroy. | Flip.

CHEAP POPULAR NOVELS, *continued*—
BY ROBERT BUCHANAN.
The Shadow of the Sword. | The Martyrdom of Madeline.
A Child of Nature. | Annan Water.
God and the Man. | The New Abelard.
Love Me for Ever.

BY MRS. BURNETT.
Surly Tim.

BY MRS. LOVETT CAMERON.
Deceivers Ever. | Juliet's Guardian.

BY MACLAREN COBBAN.
The Cure of Souls.

BY C. ALLSTON COLLINS.
The Bar Sinister.

BY WILKIE COLLINS.
Antonina. | The New Magdalen.
Basil. | The Frozen Deep.
Hide and Seek. | Law and the Lady.
The Dead Secret. | The Two Destinies
Queen of Hearts. | Haunted Hotel.
My Miscellanies. | The Fallen Leaves.
Woman in White. | Jezebel's Daughter
The Moonstone. | The Black Robe.
Man and Wife. | Heart and Science
Poor Miss Finch.
Miss or Mrs. ?

BY MORTIMER COLLINS.
Sweet Anne Page. | From Midnight to Midnight.
Transmigration.
A Fight with Fortune.

MORTIMER & FRANCES COLLINS.
Sweet and Twenty | Frances.
Blacksmith and Scholar.
The Village Comedy.
You Play me False.

BY DUTTON COOK.
Leo. | Paul Foster's Daughter.

BY WILLIAM CYPLES.
Hearts of Gold.

BY ALPHONSE DAUDET.
The Evangelist; or, Port Salvation.

BY DE MILLE.
A Castle in Spain.

BY J. LEITH DERWENT.
Our Lady of Tears. | Circe's Lovers.

BY CHARLES DICKENS.
Sketches by Boz. | Oliver Twist.
Pickwick Papers. | Nicholas Nickleby

BY MRS. ANNIE EDWARDES.
A Point of Honour. | Archie Lovell.

BY M. BETHAM-EDWARDS.
Felicia. | Kitty.

BY EDWARD EGGLESTON.
Roxy.

CHEAP POPULAR NOVELS, *continued*—
BY PERCY FITZGERALD.
Bella Donna. | Never Forgotten
The Second Mrs. Tillotson.
Polly.
Seventy-five Brooke Street.
The Lady of Brantome.

BY ALBANY DE FONBLANQUE.
Filthy Lucre.

BY R. E. FRANCILLON.
Olympia. | Queen Cophetua
One by One. | A Real Queen.

Prefaced by Sir H. BARTLE FRERE.
Pandurang Hari.

BY HAIN FRISWELL.
One of Two.

BY EDWARD GARRETT
The Capel Girls.

BY CHARLES GIBBON.
Robin Gray. | Queen of the Meadow.
For Lack of Gold.
What will the | The Flower of the World Say? | Forest.
In Honour Bound. | A Heart's Problem
The Dead Heart. | The Braes of Yarrow.
In Love and War.
For the King. | The Golden Shaft.
In Pastures Green | Of High Degree.

BY WILLIAM GILBERT.
Dr. Austin's Guests.
The Wizard of the Mountain.
James Duke.

BY JAMES GREENWOOD.
Dick Temple.

BY ANDREW HALLIDAY.
Every-Day Papers.

BY LADY DUFFUS HARDY.
Paul Wynter's Sacrifice.

BY THOMAS HARDY.
Under the Greenwood Tree.

BY JULIAN HAWTHORNE.
Garth. | Sebastian Strome
Ellice Quentin. | Dust.
Prince Saroni's Wife.
Fortune's Fool.
Beatrix Randolph.

BY SIR ARTHUR HELPS.
Ivan de Biron.

BY TOM HOOD.
A Golden Heart.

BY MRS. GEORGE HOOPER.
The House of Raby.

BY VICTOR HUGO.
The Hunchback of Notre Dame

CHEAP POPULAR NOVELS, continued—
BY MRS. ALFRED HUNT.
Thornicroft's Model.
The Leaden Casket.
Self-Condemned.

BY JEAN INGELOW.
Fated to be Free.

BY HARRIETT JAY.
The Dark Colleen.
The Queen of Connaught.

BY HENRY KINGSLEY.
Oakshott Castle. | Number Seventeen.

BY E. LYNN LINTON.
Patricia Kemball.
The Atonement of Leam Dundas.
The World Well Lost.
Under which Lord?
With a Silken Thread.
The Rebel of the Family.
"My Love!" | Ione.

BY HENRY W. LUCY.
Gideon Fleyce.

BY JUSTIN McCARTHY, M.P.
Dear Lady Disdain.
The Waterdale Neighbours.
My Enemy's Daughter.
A Fair Saxon.
Linley Rochford.
Miss Misanthrope.
Donna Quixote.
The Comet of a Season.
Maid of Athens.

BY GEORGE MAC DONALD.
Paul Faber, Surgeon.
Thomas Wingfold, Curate.

BY MRS. MACDONELL.
Quaker Cousins.

BY KATHARINE S. MACQUOID.
The Evil Eye. | Lost Rose.

BY W. H. MALLOCK.
The New Republic.

BY FLORENCE MARRYAT.
Open! Sesame!
A Harvest of Wild Oats.
A Little Stepson.
Fighting the Air.
Written in Fire.

BY J. MASTERMAN.
Half-a-dozen Daughters.

BY JEAN MIDDLEMASS.
Touch and Go. | Mr. Dorillion.

BY D. CHRISTIE MURRAY.
A Life's Atonement.
A Model Father.
Joseph's Coat.
Coals of Fire.
By the Gate of the Sea.
Val Strange.
Hearts.

BY MRS. OLIPHANT.
Whiteladies.

CHEAP POPULAR NOVELS, continued—
BY MRS. ROBERT O'REILLY.
Phœbe's Fortunes.

BY OUIDA.
Held in Bondage.
Strathmore.
Chandos.
Under Two Flags.
Idalia.
Cecil Castlemaine.
Tricotrin.
Puck.
Folle Farine.
A Dog of Flanders.
Pascarel.
Signa.
Two Little Wooden Shoes.
In a Winter City.
Ariadne.
Friendship.
Moths.
Pipistrello.
A Village Commune.
Bimbi.
In Maremma.
Wanda.
Frescoes.

BY MARGARET AGNES PAUL.
Gentle and Simple.

BY JAMES PAYN.
Lost Sir Massingberd.
A Perfect Treasure.
Bentinck's Tutor.
Murphy's Master.
A County Family.
At Her Mercy.
A Woman's Vengeance.
Cecil's Tryst.
Clyffards of Clyffe.
The Family Scapegrace.
Foster Brothers.
Found Dead.
Best of Husbands.
Walter's Word.
Halves.
Fallen Fortunes.
What He Cost Her.
Humorous Stories.
Gwendoline's Harvest.
£200 Reward.
Like Father, Like Son.
A Marine Residence.
Married Beneath Him.
Mirk Abbey.
Not Wooed, but Won.
Less Black than We're Painted.
By Proxy.
Under One Roof.
High Spirits.
Carlyon's Year.
A Confidential Agent.
Some Private Views.
From Exile.
A Grape from a Thorn.
For Cash Only.
Kit: A Memory.
The Canon's Ward.

BY EDGAR A. POE.
The Mystery of Marie Roget.

BY E. C. PRICE.
Valentina.
The Foreigners.
Mrs. Lancaster's Rival.

BY CHARLES READE.
It is Never Too Late to Mend.
Hard Cash.
Peg Woffington.
Christie Johnstone.

CHEAP POPULAR NOVELS, *continued*—
By CHARLES READE, *continued*.
Griffith Gaunt.
Put Yourself in His Place.
The Double Marriage.
Love Me Little, Love Me Long.
Foul Play.
The Cloister and the Hearth.
The Course of True Love.
Autobiography of a Thief.
A Terrible Temptation.
The Wandering Heir.
A Simpleton.
A Woman-Hater.
Readiana.
Singleheart and Doubleface.
Good Stories of Men and other Animals.
The Jilt.

BY MRS. J. H. RIDDELL.
Her Mother's Darling.
Prince of Wales's Garden Party.
Weird Stories.
The Uninhabited House.
Fairy Water.

BY F. W. ROBINSON.
Women are Strange.
The Hands of Justice.

BY W. CLARK RUSSELL.
Round the Galley Fire.

BY BAYLE ST. JOHN.
A Levantine Family.

BY GEORGE AUGUSTUS SALA.
Gaslight and Daylight.

BY JOHN SAUNDERS.
Bound to the Wheel.
One Against the World.
Guy Waterman.
The Lion in the Path.
Two Dreamers.

BY KATHARINE SAUNDERS.
Joan Merryweather.
Margaret and Elizabeth.
Gideon's Rock.
The High Mills.

BY ARTHUR SKETCHLEY.
A Match in the Dark.

BY T. W. SPEIGHT.
The Mysteries of Heron Dyke.

BY R. A. STERNDALE.
The Afghan Knife.

BY R. LOUIS STEVENSON.
New Arabian Nights.

BY BERTHA THOMAS.
Cressida. | Proud Maisie.
The Violin-Player.

BY W. MOY THOMAS.
A Fight for Life.

BY WALTER THORNBURY.
Tales for the Marines.

CHEAP POPULAR NOVELS, *continued*—
BY T. ADOLPHUS TROLLOPE.
Diamond Cut Diamond.

BY ANTHONY TROLLOPE.
The Way We Live Now.
The American Senator.
Frau Frohmann.
Marion Fay.
Kept in the Dark.
Mr. Scarborough's Family.
The Land-Leaguers.
The Golden Lion of Granpere.
John Caldigate.

By FRANCES ELEANOR TROLLOPE
Like Ships upon the Sea.
Anne Furness.
Mabel's Progress.

BY IVAN TURGENIEFF, &c.
Stories from Foreign Novelists.

BY MARK TWAIN.
Tom Sawyer.
An Idle Excursion.
A Pleasure Trip on the Continent of Europe.
A Tramp Abroad.
The Stolen White Elephant.

BY C. C. FRASER-TYTLER.
Mistress Judith.

BY SARAH TYTLER.
What She Came Through.
The Bride's Pass.

BY J. S. WINTER.
Cavalry Life. | Regimental Legends.

BY LADY WOOD.
Sabina.

BY EDMUND YATES.
Castaway. | The Forlorn Hope.
Land at Last.

ANONYMOUS.
Paul Ferroll.
Why Paul Ferroll Killed his Wife.

Fcap. 8vo, picture covers, 1s. each.
Jeff Briggs's Love Story. By BRET HARTE.
The Twins of Table Mountain. By BRET HARTE.
Mrs. Gainsborough's Diamonds. By JULIAN HAWTHORNE.
Kathleen Mavourneen. By Author of "That Lass o' Lowrie's."
Lindsay's Luck. By the Author of "That Lass o' Lowrie's."
Pretty Polly Pemberton. By the Author of "That Lass o' Lowrie's."
Trooping with Crows. By Mrs. PIRKIS.
The Professor's Wife. By LEONARD GRAHAM.
A Double Bond. By LINDA VILLARI.
Esther's Glove. By R. E. FRANCILLON.
The Garden that Paid the Rent. By TOM JERROLD.

www.ingramcontent.com/pod-product-compliance
Lightning Source LLC
Chambersburg PA
CBHW020100170426
43199CB00009B/345